The Circle Continues

Women Respond to
CIRCLE OF STONES

Gathered by Judith Duerk

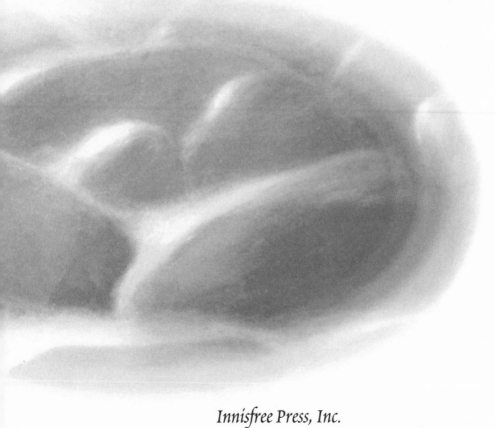

Innisfree Press, Inc.

Published by Innisfree Press, Inc.
136 Roumfort Road
Philadelphia, PA 19119-1632
800-367-5872
Visit our website at www.InnisfreePress.com

Cover design by Hugh Duffy, PhD Design
Carneys Point, New Jersey
(856-299-3316, hugh@phddesign.com)

Library of Congress Cataloging-in-Publication Data
The Circle continues : women respond to Circle of stones /
gathered by Judith Duerk
p. cm.
ISBN 1-880913-50-X
1. Women—Literary collections. 2. American literature—Women
authors. 3. Female friendship—Literary collections. I. Duerk, Judith. II. Duerk,
Judith. Circle of stones.
PS509.W6 C57 2001
810.8'0352042—dc21
2001038389

This book is dedicated to all women,

who keep making stunning differences in the world

through acts large and small.

We pay tribute to your willingness to share your experience.

—The Publisher

In celebration of the 10th anniversary

of Judith Duerk's best-selling *Circle of Stones,*

Innisfree Press issued a worldwide "call for writing and art,"

inviting women to share their stories.

In particular, we asked women to respond to the question,

"How has the affirming, sustaining presence of women

made a difference in your life?"

Selected from respondents around the world,

the pieces appearing in this book

represent the depth and beauty of a woman's journey.

Foreword

*I*t began more than a dozen years ago. A woman here, a woman there, a poem, a brief story, of a woman and her mother, or her daughter, her sisters, perhaps. Women writing in response to an image that had emerged within me over the course of the few years before that. It was an image of a circle of women, always there, present to a woman through every stage of her life. A circle of women waiting, witnessing . . . ready to receive a woman whenever she needed to feel her connection to her deepest roots in the Feminine.

When the image first came to me, I wondered if that circle was imprinted in the most profound awareness held within each woman. A very young part wanted to believe that the image was only for me, but knew that should not be. It flowed into *Circle of Stones* and *I Sit Listening To The Wind.* After the writing, I met with circles, large and small, throughout the United States and abroad.

As each woman in these circles spoke, with glowing face and shining eyes, I sensed a truth about my earlier wonderings . . . that the circles of women around her are only a reflection of the image so deeply imprinted in every woman's heart. That when that image awakens within a woman, or we awaken it within each other, it becomes the woman's task to devotedly bring it to form and to express it in her life. That these expressions brought forth from all women become the flowering of the Feminine Self.

And now this beautiful outpouring from women everywhere, bringing to form and expressing so bountifully what the image has meant for them and how it has manifested in their lives. Surely this lovely flowering from women all over the world carries the very essence, the seed that will ensure that the image of the circle of women will never, never die. For with every line, every nuance, the image is reawakened in the hearts of us all.

Let the circle continue!

—Judith Duerk

"How might your life have been different if,

through every stage of your life . . .

birth, puberty, adulthood, old age . . .

you had been received, affirmed, sustained

by a 'circle' of older, wiser women?"

—Judith Duerk, *Circle of Stones*

Table of Contents

Section 3

WOMEN'S CIRCLES

Section 4

WOMEN'S WISDOM . . . WOMEN'S VISION

Section 5

MY JOURNEY AS A WOMAN

Section 6
WOMEN'S GENERATIVITY

icons
by *Kathleen Hurt*
Appomattox, Virginia

*Y*ou surround me—
feminine icons,
essences of divinity—
hands, feet, arms, breasts;
gentle-featured faces
that have no voice
in this man-fashioned world.

I can't see you
or hear you always,
but as sure as sun rises and sets;
as sure as moon dances
in the purple-black sky,
you are here
calling me to the dance!

Your primal voices
quicken something ancient,
and I am soon lost
in the familiar melody,
swaying unconsciously
as my body enters the rhythm
of my soul.

Oh woman!
Blessed are you in all creation!
You are grace, mercy,
compassion, strength,
artist and participant
in the mystery of life.

to all the women who have influenced my life

A woman of passion . . . for painting, prose, poetry, and song, as well as those in her life and heart, Kathleen Hurt delights in coloring outside the lines. At forty-five, she considers her four grown daughters to be her greatest accomplishment thus far. Kathleen plans to spend the rest of her life dancing to the rhythm of her soul, while encouraging women of all ages to join her.

Section 1

*My Mother,
My Grandmother . . .
My Sisters, Aunts, and Cousins*

Alpha's Circle of Stones
by Alpha McClellan-Gibson
Asheville, North Carolina

*T*his particular circle of stones came into being December 1993 . . . after forty-eight years of being my mother's daughter, forty-eight years of being abused by and distrustful of and distant from her, I opened my heart to my mother who was dying of cancer three thousand miles away. From this distance, I felt it was safe to love and to forgive, and we started spending several hours a week on the phone together. We learned more about each other in the last fourteen months of her life than all the years previous. Finally, we could laugh and cry with each other; finally, we could be open and honest.

In 1993, my mother asked me what I wanted for Christmas. I told her that I had everything I needed or wanted, but she seemed to really want to send me something. So I told her I would love to have a few of those beautiful stones I had seen when I had taken her to my brother Alan's house the past spring.

"Stones, Alpha?"

"Stones, Mama. I love stones."

So, one of her last physical activities was to sit outside with a small trowel and slowly dig up stones from my brother's flower beds and carefully wash them off. My brother boxed and shipped them from Oregon to Mississippi, one-hundred pounds of stones from my eighty-five pound mother. A true gift of love.

Her health rapidly deteriorated, and she passed from this earth in July 1994. We brought her home to Alabama to be buried next to our father.

Thirty-six of "her stones," arranged in a circle on my entry floor, stand as evidence for all who enter my home to see . . . what Mother and I had learned . . . that life, like love, is a circle.

Alpha McClellan-Gibson is a world traveler on her spiritual journey, recently divorced, and living with her "best buddy" of eleven years—a Himalayan cat called "Katie." Alpha and her beloved, Will, are currently seeking their "perfect place" in the much-loved Smoky Mountains. Alpha's "Circle of Stones" is at home wherever she lives.

Touchstones
by Sylvia Cornette
Forsyth, Missouri

Once we were a clan of women. There were men in our lives, but they hovered on the periphery. They came to the fore of our lives on the Fourth of July when they cranked the ice cream freezer and set off the fireworks. They can be seen at the edges of the pictures pasted in the family album. They were behind the camera, orchestrating our lives, but they never determined our destinies. Those were determined by the laughing faces of the young women outlined for all time by the margins around the family pictures.

That is the way I remember us: laughing. When I think of one, I think of all of us together. We numbered twelve. We were all female, the progeny of five sisters. Faithfully, we gathered twice every year. The site of our pilgrimage was the farm home of our aunt.

Although our days together were busy, I do not remember the specifics. What lingers in memory is our nighttime ritual. The large tin tub was placed in the kitchen and partially filled with warm water. One by one, the cousins would bathe, each one adding hot water until by the end of the twelfth bath, the tub was full of soapy, gray water.

While we were bathing, our mothers would spread quilts and pillows the length of the main room of the house to create one big pallet where we slept. As we finished our baths and slipped into our nightclothes, we began to negotiate where we would sleep. There was much stepping over each other until everyone found a spot. Those of similar age slept snuggled next to each other, bracketed by younger or older cousins.

There were at least two heads on each pillow, and one quilt covered several small bodies. We shared. We didn't fight, but we did learn to hang on to our part of the quilt during the night! The heat of bodies warmed us physically and spiritually. It was comforting to touch someone, no matter which way we turned in the darkness. There was some whispering under cover of the quilt, but we did not whisper too much. Twelve girls fell silent. We were quiet in order to hear our mothers talk. This was our chance to hear the conversation of adults.

They gathered around the dining table at the far end of the room. The light from the kitchen illuminated their cups of coffee. Ideas filled the air. They collided with each other and were transformed into new ideas, knowledge. Our mothers were talented, accomplished women. They were educated and had careers as teachers and principals of schools before their marriages, in a time and place when it was unseemly for married women to be in the classroom. Their careers were terminated by marriage, but their independence was not. It was transmitted to the twelve girls who slept at their feet.

Our mothers celebrated their womanhood. They celebrated ours.

Knowledge was important to each of the sisters, and they each had strong ideas. They might vehemently argue, but there was one thing about which they all agreed: They agreed on the importance of family stories in their lives and ours. Their conversation would soon transition from ideas and knowledge to family history, our roots.

Listening to those late night conversations, we learned of those who had gone before us. We knew who had curly hair, who had red hair, who was musically talented. We learned who we were and our place in the family. We learned what was expected of us. We knew we were to value our minds and our education, and we were subtly taught to create lives of our own.

We learned about life from those late-night family stories. We understood that we were to use the stories to guide us in our lives. We listened to the cadence of the soft voices telling the oft-repeated stories until our eyes and ears grew heavy. We fell asleep with the lullaby of stories ringing in our ears.

The twelve girls have scattered, but we carry those stories in our memory, in our hearts. They bind us. We have shared them with the next generation, our own daughters. Our mothers' stories always will be a part of our being.

Sylvia Cornette is a wife, mother and grandmother whose life has been shaped by her family, friends, and strangers met while traveling who became friends. She values experiences with people more than positions she has held or possessions she owns. A disaster in the kitchen, she takes solace by nourishing souls through the gift of story.

Homes Have Long Memories
by Yvonne Mokihana Calizar
Honolulu, Hawaii

I have come home to Kuliouou to rebuild a place that once helped to build me.

As a girl I was comfortable with the small stones that lay in scatters on the red-brown dirt beneath the hibiscus hedges and fruit trees. My friends and I created our world of simple homes and walls laid in outlines using those little stones. We laughed, imitating the lives of women who shared their way of being with us.

The women of Kuliouou made room for tiny girls. They were the birthing stones like the *pohaku of Ka`u*, the stones found on the shores of Ka`u on the island of Hawaii. These smooth stones are covered with pin-sized openings. As these stones sit in the wetness of salt-water, grains of gray-black sand fall from the openings or *puka* and slowly gather alongside the mother stones. The Hawaiian has always known that we humans are always in the company of family. Our ancestors are the stones, the *pohaku*. The stones of Ka`u are more commonly called *pohaku li`ili`i hanau* or stones that give birth to smaller stones.

Two women of Kuliouou Valley, in times not so long ago, were the *pohaku* of my life. My mother, Helen Mokihana Calizar, was a lei-maker, a daughter of a lei-seller. Her fingers were long and tapered, with thick bluntly cut nails that ended just beyond the tops of each fingertip. She held the fragile buds of jasmine as she gathered a palm full of sweet pikake blossoms. When she was making a lei, she performed her rituals of gatherings without ceremony or pomp. Freshly maturing blossoms were ready in the earliest of morning light, when dew still rested on the small leaves and sun was still softly stretching itself over the ridges. It could take a week of mornings to gather enough blossoms to string two ropes of the precious pikake for a graduation gift. Day after day, she would rest selected blooms in a moist fold of paper towels in the refrigerator. In different seasons, the paper towel bundles changed—pikake, white ginger, and gardenia.

For forty years Ma lived just the other side of the red hibiscus and mock-orange hedge from my Aunty Lily. From my side of the hedge, I knew when Aunty Lily was out back feeding the bunny or scooping rain-water from her rain buckets—from the sounds of rubber slippers slapping the soles of feet. If her slippers were silent for more than a few counts . . . one, two, three, four . . . I knew she had hunkered down over her feet and was up to something good!

"Hi, Aunty Lily," I'd call through the hedge, waiting for her to ask me over to be included in her daily round of stuff-going-on-today. The *puka*, a hole the size of one small person, arched between the hedge. It has always been the portal between the yards. My small, almost always bare, feet etched a path across Aunty Lily's backyard. For scores of days, nights, and years Yurie Tanaka Buffins was my neighbor, craft-master, botanist, and translator of clouds. I learned to notice life's happenings in miniature while squatting next to her. She always wore the darkest of green sunglasses night and day. A blue bandana enveloped her long, straight black hair, except where the very deliberate curve of hair was pinned over one side of her face. It hid a deep scar. A chicken pox scar. I never knew that as a child, never thought to ask, didn't need to know.

Inside Aunty Lily's house I discovered the amazing effect books, print, magazines, and newspapers could have on the spirit of a small girl. The two-bedroom cottage was always stuffed with bookshelves filled with hardcover books, *My Book House* books, *Childcraft*, and *Guidepost* Magazines. Newspaper towers rose from the floor wherever there was room. Clippings from old *Honolulu Advertiser* and *Star-Bulletin* newspapers lay under glass paperweights with dates and other pencil scribblings in the corner. Sometimes the clippings were stuck into envelopes. Someone, somewhere was going to read these words again. Nothing went unread or unused. After we read the newsprint, the paper became weed-stopping mulch and walkways during the rainy seasons in Kuliouou Valley.

Aunty Lily liked me just the way I was. Whatever I said was just right, and if the night had passed badly in our house, she always knew it . . . but let the feelings find their place in the new day, never prying into my sadness or bubble of quiet. Without knowing it, I was learning that things pass. Everything passes. She could turn a changing cloudscape into a lesson about things unseen but no less real. From the shade of the soursap tree, she'd stop, bend over with a sickle, and shift her head upward at the sky over Kuliouou: "See . . . God is taking the sheep home." Out of the quiet of many afternoons, I was reminded that I was never really alone.

At twenty-four I felt the crimp of a pot too tight against my sprouting roots, and in more ways than a fist-full, I cracked the vessel, left the *ohana* family, and wandered. The Hawaiian word for wandering is *auana*, and it is the word parents use to describe young people who stray. Wandering is a kind of thing some people are born to do. My life has taken me thousands of miles from the old home place. Yet the patient gathering practices of a lei-maker had seeped deep into my reality. "There is time for everything, `auana* girl. In time, you will learn this for yourself." And the seeds of belief have helped me find my gift. After I married and moved away, Aunty Lily read my letters and told me I was a good writer. I believed her, and I kept writing.

The teachers who had begun their work with me while I was a young girl of Kuliouou now began to tell me in my daydreams and my nightdreams, "It's your turn."

I came home to Kuliouou to rebuild a home, and it in turn has reminded me that the home will continue to rebuild me. The memories of time rest in the wood of my old house, now painted a warm butter yellow. Fresh coats of pastel cover the redwood walls throughout the 1950s Hicks home my parents built. Hibiscus curtains flop in the wind and mimic the fresh red blossoms that dangle on branches just outside the louvered kitchen windows. A family of special *pohaku li`ili`i hanau* lives in a clear etched glass bowl that had been my mother's. Pete has trimmed the windows with cedar. Blue and sage paint accents play tricks on the eye as the light changes during the day, creating another *pu`olo* sacred bundle for collecting daily memories.

My straight black hair now sparkles with silver. At fifty-years old, my pace has slowed and my senses sharpened. I am now learning that becoming an elder involves much more than having gray hair and grandchildren. I am learning the ancient practice of *makua o`o*, which, literally translated, means maturing adult with a digging stick. I respond to the *kahea* or call to become more and more myself. For me, *kahea* means a commitment to writing. I have begun writing a regular column called *Makua o`o*, and in it I share my practice that is my daily life. Each time I write I remember the basic life tools of *Makua o`o*:

- keep a keen sense of observation
- listen with your whole body
- do your best in all things
- know that wisdom is found in many places
- question for clarity when making decisions
- practice patience and endurance
- engage in good health practices
- feel the heartbeat of the culture
- believe in *Ke Akua*, for this higher power makes all life possible

I am home where *tutus* grandparents and aunties, cousins and next-door neighbors taught me to clear space for dreams, swiftly changing cloudscapes, and broad mind. It is no accident that my forehead is high, wide and curved . . . like the earth honua. As I practice the *o`o*, I am learning to ask questions and hear the answers in the drip of a winter rain, or the stillness of a calm night. When it is time to die, I hope my life tools, my *o'o,* will be worn from use.

Yvonne Mokihana Calizar is a writer and columnist living on the island of Oahu, in Hawaii, where she also teaches gentle yoga to students of all ages and stages of life. She and her life partner, Pete, chose to return to her family home four years ago to rebuild and rescue it from termites and neglect, and in the process they are learning what to keep and what to throw out of their lives.

A Daughter's Tribute to Her Mother
by Catherine R. Duffy
St. George, Bermuda

As a young girl, I seem to recall that life was perfect. I had a very loving mother who was always there when I needed her. My father was the provider. Therefore, he was never really there. But he did not need to be because my mother was the core of the family. She provided us with our foundation, our beliefs, and our direction.

I remember the times when my mother was full of wit. I remember when she used to hide behind walls draped in a white sheet to jump out to scare us. I can still see her shrieking with laughter. I can still see the happiness spread across her face.

I also see the woman who was a naturalist before it was trendy to be a naturalist. I thank her for all of the natural products that she would prepare for us. Every Sunday, she gave us Citric Milk of Magnesia just to keep our blood pure. We were never allowed to drink plain water. She mixed our water with flaxseed or aloe to purify our blood. She never took us to restaurants because she did not feel they were clean enough for us. She always prepared fresh baked breads, cookies, and home-cooked meals. She believed in nothing artificial. Funny how, back then, I believed we were poor because I used to go to school with big thick slices of home-baked bread when everyone else had "Sunbeam Bread."

It was not until I became a woman myself that I realized deep down inside that I knew she was not perfect. To the outside world, she appeared to be strong, independent, and beautiful, so full of life. To those of us, who were exposed to the true Adele Clithrow Harvey Johnstone, we knew these things to be untrue. All her life, she looked for recognition, she looked for love. She was a woman of many dreams.

When she met Erskine Edward Fraser Swan, a hard-working, handsome young man, she felt she had been rescued. Here was a man ready to accept her with two little girls in tow, my older sisters, Pat and Pam, who had been conceived from her first and second boyfriends, respectively. Yet she missed all the signs. Her prince charming had grown up in an abusive environment. He had to quit school at the age of thirteen in order to help his mother to survive. His father died at a very young age due to his excessive drinking, and my father had to grow up fast, without being shown much love.

But she felt she had finally hit the jackpot. He wined and dined her. He gave her flowers and chocolates. He told her she was beautiful. She was caught up in the whirlwind. So much so she forgot to observe his environment. She was blinded by love.

They married and he took her on her dream honeymoon. Life was good. She was so happy. But within weeks, the honeymoon ended. They had returned from heaven to move in with her father. They were never able to have the intimacy needed to build a young marriage.

Because of my father's home environment and the era in which he was born, he was a man driven to make as much money as he could in order to provide for his family. This was the only way he knew how to show he cared. He was a man with as many scars as my mother. He felt he would bring shame to his name if he allowed his wife to work. He felt he had to be in full control of the household regardless of the consequences. As a result, my mother was never allowed to work. She was never allowed to learn to drive. She was forced to lose herself.

To feel she had accomplished something as a woman, she bore four more children. Erskine, Eddie, Chris, and I were her accomplishments during her marriage to my father. Her children were her world. She lived her dreams through them.

My father, sensing something was lacking in their lives, decided it was time to move the family from my mother's homestead to our own. He had secretly bought a home and had been renting it out so that the mortgage payments would be more manageable when we moved into it. For a while, both my mother and father were feeling as if they had accomplished something together. We were finally a family in our own home. A place where we could put up our own Christmas tree. A place we could always call home.

We were perfect, but not for long. On the surface, the house was always full of the smell of fresh baked goods. Mama was always there. But slowly the scabs were falling off to reveal the sores, the old realities, and the buried pain.

After Chris was born, my mother attempted to commit suicide. She was desperately looking for help, but though the family rallied around her, she could not freely admit she needed help. Instead, we dusted her off and sent her to live with my father's sister for a while instead of sending her to the psychiatric hospital she so desperately needed.

The downward spiral began for her. Slowly, she was losing herself. Instead of admitting her true feelings because she feared she would shame her family, she bottled them all up inside. Her blood pressure rose. Silently, she was killing herself.

I remember one hot day coming home from school, and there was my mother walking down the street in a wool coat and a woolen hat. I could have died. All my friends were around so I pretended I did not see her. I waited until she was out of sight before I walked home. Actually, I ran so she would not catch up with me. I was only thirteen; I did not understand she needed help.

Sometimes I would come home and find her lying on the couch, covering her whole body even though it was hot outside. The next day, she would be walking around half-clothed because she was so hot. I always thought she was whining because she was not the strong woman I was used to seeing. She was crumbling before my eyes, and I did not know how to deal with it.

My most vivid memories of my mother are the last few days of her life. The first true sign of trouble came one week before she died. She was lying in bed with me when, all of a sudden, she sat up, shaking uncontrollably with sweat pouring down her face. She was crying. She jumped out of bed. She looked as if she had seen a ghost.

I immediately started to cry because I could see and feel her pain. I asked her what was wrong.

She answered, "I thought that I was dead."

I cried harder. She then calmed down because she realized she had frightened me.

"Don't worry," she said. "Everything is going to be okay. It was only a dream. I am not going to die." Shivering, she got back into bed and hugged me.

I believed her. I believed everything was okay.

The night before my mother had her stroke, she was coming to bed with me as she normally did. However, on this night, she wanted to bring my brother Chris with her. Chris was only seven years old at the time, and he still wet his bed on occasion. I did not want him in bed with me, so I told her he had to go back to his own bed.

That night Chris was unusually clingy to my mother. He did not want to leave her side. So my mother went to her own bed and took Chris with her.

Three hours later my father was waking us all and saying, "Come look at your mother. This will probably be the last time you see her."

I can still feel the same sensation I felt that night. I thought my father was crazy for waking us. He called my sister, Pat, who is a nurse's assistant, to come to the house to see my mother and figure out what was wrong with her. She was snoring loudly. There was froth coming from her mouth. She was half clothed.

The ambulance arrived. They put her on the stretcher. I felt as if we were all moving in slow motion. The dog was howling. All of the children were gathered around not looking at each other nor uttering one word. We were all frozen in our own thoughts. It was and will always be the strangest feeling I would ever experience in my life.

The next day, May 18, 1976, my mother suffered a cerebral brain hemorrhage and never regained consciousness. She died without saying good-bye.

On March 15, 1999, I became a new mother. It is only now that I can fully appreciate and respect the woman my mother chose to be. She had created her own world, a world where she could find solace when life became too much for her to bear. She was trying to be the best mother and woman she could be, given her circumstances. She had also been showing all of the classic signs of someone about to have a stroke. She was beginning to lose her memory. She was becoming very moody.

In 1976, this information was not as freely available as it is now. In those days, people just thought she was losing her mind.

As a thirteen-year-old, I had been angry at her. How could she have lied to me? How dare she leave me so unexpectedly? She had told me she would stay with me, and she did not. We had never discussed what the consequences of her death would be. We would never become woman friends. I resented her for living what I thought was such a pointless life. I resented her for allowing a man to control her. I resented her for never becoming the woman I thought she was so capable of becoming.

Oh, Mama, if only you would have let me in. Maybe we could have helped each other. Maybe things would be different now. Maybe. Maybe. Maybe . . .

Catherine Rochelle Duffy is a free-lance writer and author, and self-proclaimed Domestic Goddess, who lives on the beautiful paradise island of Bermuda with her husband, Nick, and son, Raven. Since the birth of her son, she has completely changed her life, leaving a high profile corporate career to dedicate her time to her family and writing.

My Aunt
by Peggy Sapphire
Craftsbury, Vermont

I hoped she'd never lose weight, this round aunt
of mine, fair skinned, blue-eyed, freckle-faced woman
whose delight in clothes was color, with the flair of flags
she'd wrap robes and gowns across herself. But to me,
nothing mattered more than that she heard my call,
my voice, with the pleasure of being my aunt.

I wanted her big and bosomy, wanted her
slow moving, patient, and smiling as she served up
portions of foods my mother never approved. I wanted her
to insist on second helpings, or more, to reckon my shyness
about another slice of brisket or fruit pie.

I counted on her being free for my visit whenever I
could get away, whenever I needed to cry
at her Formica table which fit into her kitchen
only if it was never moved away from the wall,
worn from green to gray from decades and generations
of all of us gathering there when we needed her.

I carried her presence in my life like my only
key. When all else failed me, a bed made for decent
sleep, late and warm, a lamp to guide my nightly journaling,
a place at meals with cousins all around, my uncle presiding,
this family without jealousy that I had come needing,
circling me like a woolen shawl still warm from their bodies.

Once my aunt had a mother of her own, a father, a home
in the city of the most famous waltz of all. But Vienna in 1938
became a nightmare, and its train tracks ran molten with
transports carrying new orphans west to London, and
cattle cars north to Buchenwald, Theresienstadt, and Dachau.

A pale thirteen-year-old girl, her blue eyes blind with tears,
groped among the faces of other sobbing kinder for any
who could comfort or explain. There were none.
No words for ripping her child-heart, still breathing Mother. Mother.
No words for the fractured fingers of her father's outstretched hands.
No words for metal doors slamming on her ashen face wrecked with terror.

Deposited in a London orphanage, warehoused, claimed,
given over as a live-in, a girl without choices,
who saved her tears for pillows in a little attic room.
She obeyed, hoarded wages to fund her parents' rescue, believing
for years though their letters were long ceased, disbelieving
the cataclysm, finally collapsed, lit a candle
and never said another prayer.

This woman swore never to break a child's heart, never
to abandon, never to deprive, never to frighten. This woman
cried in the arms of a good man who had the gift of listening,
who welcomed her home. This woman's bosom grew full
with milk for all her babies, whose tiny fingerings of her
mouth and eyes were mapping gentleness, comfort,
her gaze lit from within.

My aunt survived terrors she does not, cannot yet, may never reveal.
A trace of a distant language remains. She paints canvases of broad, huge
flowers filling the walls in her home with the colors of her clothes,
I see that now. Unfolding eternal blossoms as memorials to those
whose last embrace survived with her, or else she would long ago
have annihilated
herself.

I fear life without her yet I would not dare to do less than she,
would not break the circle she has carried,
has drawn around me.

My daughter calls to me.

I am here. I hear you.
I am here.
Always here.

*Peggy Sapphire lives and writes in the Northeast Kingdom of Vermont. Her poetry
and short fiction have appeared in various literary journals. Beginning in the Fall
2001, she will become the new Editor of Connecticut Poetry Review, a national poetry
journal. She is a member of the International Women's Writing Guild, Connecticut
Poetry Society, and New England Writers. It was these circles of friendship that
brought word of Judith Duerk's call for submissions to* The Circle Continues.

Happy Birthday
by Joan Alagna
Brooklyn, New York

How do you write a story about one of the most significant people in your life? I guess you begin at the beginning.

As was the custom in Italian families, a child was named for their grandmother or grandfather. This child was no exception. I was named for my maternal grandmother, Salvatrice Russo, who was to become my role model.

Salvatrice Russo was born in Militello, Sicily, on April 10, 1895. She was the daughter of Rosario Russo and Maria Stella Barone and the youngest of seventeen children, of whom only seven survived. She married my grandfather, Francesco Incivilito, who came from a neighboring town called Francofonte. My grandparents had dreams of a new life in America just like millions of immigrants before them. Together they left Italy and came to America in 1913. For these two young Sicilians, the promise of America was never realized. My grandfather died just four years later, leaving my grandmother a widow with two small children: my mother, aged two, and her brother, aged six months.

My grandmother Sadie (as she came to be called) knew what lay before her. She had to raise her children alone. She measured up to the task with courage, love, and tenacity, never losing sight of who she was, a proud and strong Italian woman. Although illiterate (as was the custom then; schooling if any, was for the boys), off she went to find a job. My gutsy grandmother not only got a sewing job that paid well, she was one of the fortunate tailors who even worked during the Depression. Grandma worked forty-four years in her trade.

Through her hard work and diligence, Grandma was able to move from the Lower East Side to Brooklyn in 1929. "*La Campania*" (the country), as she called it, became home. I still remember lots of company and good food with lots of laughter, music and dancing. Could my Grandma ever dance! She made every holiday a special one. She loved to show me off to the neighbors and particularly to her coworkers, and I loved going visiting with her. We would walk hand-in-hand amidst the smiles of people who sat on their stoops during the summer months. *"Buona sera, buona sera"* ("Good evening"), they would say. It was music to my ears.

Grandma had a way about her that is hard to describe. She was a contradiction—at times soft and earthy, tough and strong, caring and compassionate, domineering and tyrannical. She was someone who loved me as I was, no strings attached. Her unconditional love has helped shape my personality and my outlook on life. Grandma was a great teacher and yet she could be a learner, too. She went to night school, learned to read English (with a small assist from me), and became a citizen. How exciting it was for me (I was about seven at the time) to help Grandma with her homework.

Grandma had a love of flowers and the good earth. Roses grew in abundance in our back yard, along with some vegetables, especially tomatoes, and grapes to make wine. Our backyard was home to a peach tree. Grandma would make bouquets of roses which I (lucky kid!) would bring to *I cugini* (cousins) and *I paesani* (neighbors) on the block. How wonderful it was to be the flower bearer.

My Grandmother will be ninety-two-years old on April 10th. I want to and will always remember Grandma as she was. Age has a way of diminishing a person's vitality, and Grandma is no exception. Yet even now she can say to me, "I love you" and it thrills me just like it did when I was two and nine and twenty-nine. Grandma, I love you. I am proud to be your namesake.

Happy Birthday, Grandma.

Joan Alagna, a sixty-four-year-old "kid from Brooklyn" remembers growing up in Grandma's house and an extended Italian American family where women were the heart and soul of the family. A single parent, proud, mother of three wonderful children, and professional counselor, Joan wrote this story for her grandmother's birthday, only to have it read as the eulogy when she died.

Muñeca
by Rebecca Johnson
Orlando, Florida

$\mathcal{I}$t's late February, and I'm up early sitting at the old wooden café table on my small, screened-in patio sipping a well-steeped cup of ginger tea and writing slowly, laboriously in my notebook. We're having more beautiful, near perfect days this winter, "Chamber-of-Commerce weather" the local meteorologist likes to say. Mother used to call it "open-window weather" for rare are the days in Florida when you can shut off the air conditioner and open the house—all day and all night—to the balmy bay breezes. The cold monsoons of January left behind lush native ferns and wildly overgrown foliage. It's as if Madam Nature took her widest paint brush and stroked the landscape before me thick with green, greener even than our drive through the Emerald Isle's Ring of Kerry. Then She splashed on globs of purple and white azaleas in full bloom. How mother loved azaleas. Our entire side yard was lined with several giant bushes of them.

The azaleas in my garden look so beautiful now. The only thing left for me to do is hang the pots of petunias, put out the begonias, and buy some bright orange bougainvillea, things my mother and I used to do together. I'll probably cut a few hydrangeas, too, for the vase on the dining room table. The thought of these small pre-spring gardening rituals without mother pains my heart to tears. "Happy tears," she used to call them.

Maybe that's what drew me to the Hispanic market today, the little market where no one speaks English, although everyone in the store probably can. I love the noisy chatter and the familiar din. How all the women call me *chiquita* or baby, and I feel nurtured and coddled and loved. Like the petite Puerto Rican woman with the beautiful natural arch in her eyebrows and the soft moist skin who stops to help me pick out a yucca.

I decide to go eat at Gina's restaurant Delicios, *Comidas Latina y Cantina a Domicilio.* It's a small, storefront café next to the dry cleaners at the corner of Oak Ridge and Orange Avenues. The walls are part brick, part tile, part wallboard, and part unfinished.

In the center of the room surrounded by a chest-high counter stands Gina and her gas stove. As always, there are big pots of red beans and black beans cooking and lots of yellow and white rice. The familiar scent of Cuban cooking—a blend of olive oil and garlic, roast pork and onions, and espresso—fills my nostrils and clings to my clothes so it will linger with me long into the afternoon.

Gina comes out from behind her kitchen to greet me. "Hi, *muñeca,*" she whistles softly through her smile. Loosely translated, *muñeca* means "little doll" in Spanish but it is often used as an endearment for little girls, and it always takes me back to a good feeling from my childhood whenever she calls me that. I ask her if she ever makes crab rolls, but she tells me no because there are no fresh crabs in Orlando. That makes me homesick for Tampa and reminds me of the first time my mother and I bought the Latin delicacy from a downtown sidewalk vendor. We had heard about the old Cuban man and his crab rolls from all the ladies in the neighborhood and all the men at my father's office. We doused them in hot sauce and ate all that we had bought, sitting right there on the curb on the side of the street. Coming from the Midwest, we had never tasted anything like this before. I was nine years old at the time, and we'd only been in Tampa a few months.

But the old man on the corner of downtown Tampa has long since passed, and the only place to get a really good homemade crab roll anymore is at Carmine's Seventh Avenue in Ybor City. The last time I was there it was just forty-two days after my mother had died.

I had come to Carmine's Seventh Avenue that day to try and collect myself and pick up something to eat before going to Jeanne's house. Jeanne, my friend since fourth grade, had lost her mother to cancer just two years before me. Each time I stayed with her, she held my heart in her hand and let me bleed through every pore of my body as long as I needed to, gently handling me like a piece of cracked porcelain until I grew strong enough to leave and face the world for a little while longer.

Jeanne came to my mother's funeral and stood by me as I stood by the casket during the viewing. I needed to watch and listen to the good-byes. I needed to stand by my mother as she stood by me all my life. Like the time she insisted on going with me to Lake City. My husband was having emergency surgery, and I had a three-hour drive in front of me. I would not know until I got there if he would live through the surgery. I could not have made that trip without my mother's inner strength. Her osteoarthritis was so advanced, all movements—sitting, walking, even sleeping—greatly pained her, but as always, she focused on the problem before her. We slept together in one oversized bed in a motel room along the main drag, and we ate most of our meals at the Waffle House. While my husband recovered, we shopped at Wal-Mart or picked camellias. Every morning before going to the hospital, we went to the Catholic church and lit a candle, a soothing and comforting ritual left over from her Irish Catholic upbringing. Although my husband would survive his ordeal, unfortunately our marriage wouldn't. But through it all, my mother remained by my side.

That's why it was so hard for me to leave hers. I found it incredulous to see her lying there with all the pain gone from her body and anxiety drained from her face. She seemed so relaxed, so serene. I leaned down and whispered to her what she had whispered to me: "Remember the good times; remember the love." Then I felt the small, soft hand of my Aunt Ella. She smiled down at my mother and said to me, "Look at her. She looks like a little china doll."

Rebecca Johnson is a freelancer who lives and works with her two cats. She prefers writing in cafés, particularly ones that serve Cuban coffee and mofongo.

Sisterhood
by Kathleen Nizzari
New York, New York

I often refer to women as a universal sisterhood: individuals connected through a familial covenant by their very nature of being female. Having been born to a family of seven daughters (yes, seven!), I know this sisterhood from birth.

My mother inducted me into the sisterhood. She was my teacher, my guide, my voice, my nurturer. An older sister, Diana, was a woman of the world, well-traveled, career-minded, and a go-getter. As a child and young adult, I always looked up to her. My sister Christine is one year younger than I am. Because we are so close in age, we were quite close growing up. As a child and into my teens, I was very protective of Chris. Sure, we went through the typical rivalries young siblings do. Yet I can recall quite clearly certain instances where other girls would pick a fight with her and I would rush in to her rescue. Because I was a skinny little thing, I'd no doubt lose the fight, just as I knew I would going into it, but that never stopped me. The important thing was that my sister was in need and I was there to try to protect her. It never concerned me that I'd end up with bruises. That never prevented me from stepping in the next time.

As Chris and I got older, different schools, different circles of friends, different tastes and locations took us in two separate directions. Despite her being more the traditional type and I the rebel rouser, neither of us tries to mold the other to fit our own personal lifestyle. Neither of us tries to change the other. Where she is devoted to her family and has a stable home, I am a single woman who travels and runs her own business. But Chris never tries to talk me into settling down just because it is the path she has chosen. Conversely, I don't tell her she's wrong for not wanting to go on an African safari and sleep outdoors with wild animals. While these differences may be germane to who we are as individuals, they do not separate us as sisters.

For as long as I live, I shall never forget Chris's kindness and compassion when my cat of nearly eighteen years, Banshee (another member of the sisterhood), was stricken with cancer and passed on. During her stay in the hospital, I went to see her daily. On one of those days, Chris packed up her two children and headed over with me for visiting hours. Although she is not the staunch animal lover I am and does not particularly care for hospitals, Chris put aside her personal feelings and freely offered to come to support me. When Banshee passed, Chris again came to the hospital to pick us up. Knowing how difficult this time was for me, neither she nor my mother wanted me to be alone. They took care of the funeral arrangements and attended with me to pay their last respects. Never once did they try to stop my tears and say I was overreacting. They understood my pain.

What makes a sisterhood? Giving support through difficult times; rejoicing in the happiness and success of others; being honest always, even if the truth is unpleasant. It's hand holding as much as it is a pat on the back, but never is it a slap in the face.

Sisters defend one another when we're right. We tenderly help each other to see when we're wrong, but we never point fingers. When one of us gets down on herself, we don't pick up the whip for extra lashings. Nor do we take each other down through selfishness or jealousy when one of us is up. We share and are not covetous. We identify but don't compare. We are not competitive. We have faith and trust in each other to make our own decisions. We are not controlling. We have respect for one another.

My goddaughter was enrolled into this sisterhood at birth. As Chris's daughter, Victoria, begins to understand, I'd like to pass these gifts on to her. I want to nurture the fiery independence inherent in her, my fellow Aries. Not only am I her aunt, her blood relative, but I also want to be a true sister. In sisterhood, the circle continues.

Kathleen Nizzari, a native New Yorker who shares her penthouse with her two cats, recently reinvented herself in business. Her personal credo is "Respect all living beings." A vegetarian of twenty-two years, she is passionate about family, animal rights, environmental issues, and philosophy. She hopes one day to publish her collections of essays, poetry, and fiction.

Bella Nonna
by Loretta Benedetto Marvel
New Rochelle, New York

The little yellow room carved out of the eaves of the attic is where I paint, sew, journal, doodle, and restore myself through quiet meditation. When I sit at my desk, I am surrounded by my paints and papers and fabrics and rubber stamps and photos and talismans given to me by the kids and friends over the years. Lately, I've been experimenting with painting on fabric, and I decided to try out the new unbleached muslin and fabric paints that arrived in the mail today. I cut a piece of muslin about three feet wide and four feet long and stretched it onto a piece of foam core to use as an easel. I've squirted a bunch of blue and green paints onto a paper plate, and I dip a sea sponge lightly into turquoise blue and dusty green, and gently begin to sponge the fabric. I work rhythmically with the sponge, picking up paint and dabbing it this way and that onto the fabric until it becomes mottled with blue. The color is familiar to me but I can't place it. I find myself reaching for a drawing pencil and sketching a figure in the middle of the fabric. I switch the pencil for a brush and black paint, and slowly the full-bodied figure of a female appears, one arm outstretched to her head like the Statue of Liberty.

Not sure of where I am going with this, I suddenly realize that the blue of the fabric reminds me of the inside shell of the concrete grottoes to the Virgin Mary that dot the Italian neighborhoods of my hometown. The figure is definitely female and sort of resembles the Madonna, but I have an urge to paint a teapot on top of her head pouring a stream of tea into the teacup held in her outstretched hand. Around her waist an apron appears with pockets full of baking tools like spatulas and cookie cutters. A large rosary hangs from one arm and her purse from the other. Topping off her outfit is a resplendent mink stole. Above her head, I paint the words, "Bring me your hungry . . ." and around her shoulders I letter, "Bella Nonna, Kitchen Madonna."

Suddenly Jessica, my oldest daughter, appears. "Why does the Statue of Liberty have a teapot on her head? Who's Bella Nonna?"

I shrug my shoulders, "I don't know." But she sure is familiar to me. Then from somewhere inside me, the answer comes: "She's my family, well, the image of the women of my family, all the women who have gone before me and those who are yet to come." My answer surprises even me, welling up from some deep spring inside me that I was not aware of. An ancient figure, a goddess of some sort, but in the very familiar clothing of my grandmothers and great-aunts. I'm not surprised when Jessica leaves the room mumbling about how Mom's gone off her rocker, while I paint loaves of Italian bread and glasses of red wine, tart red cherries, and bundles of herbs around my Bella Nonna.

My life has always been rich in the company of women. The middle daughter of an Italian-American family, my world revolved around a constant constellation of female stars. Four sisters, a mother, two grandmothers, six aunts, several great aunts, and assorted female cousins ranging from infants to newly married, I had a wealth of feminine influence and role models to consider. At any point in my youth, a female was undergoing a rite of passage, whether giving birth, going on a first date, undergoing a hysterectomy, or getting her period for the first time. There was an eleven-year age difference between the birth of my oldest sister and the youngest, so that even in our own household, a female was usually in the throes of a major life experience, from joining the Girl Scouts to getting ready for the prom.

Our female relatives were larger than life. My mother's mother had married at fifteen and had her first child, my Aunt Anita, at sixteen. At the age of forty, she had her last child, a "change-of-life baby," as they called it back then. This was my Uncle Richard, who was a mere two years older than my oldest sister, Carol. Grandma was the matriarch of the family, a ward leader for the Republican party, a founding member of the Italian Arts Society, player of bridge and crocheter of endless yards of variegated woolen afghans. Gussie, her sister, was a telephone operator—"overseas," as my grandmother would remind us, conferring the importance of overseas over domestic calls. Gussie was also my godmother and the first woman I knew to wear pants outside the house. With her black widow's peak and deep telephone-operator voice, she was a comical figure in her full-length fur coat over her ubiquitous black polyester pants.

Our childhood lives followed the passage of the seasons, punctuated with birthday parties featuring homemade sponge cakes covered with icing roses; Thanksgivings with ravioli and a turkey; Christmases stretching into a week of visiting and eating; Easters with the dyeing of the eggs; Fourth of July picnics on our screened-in porch; the annual treks to Jones Beach, dragging the heavy metal cooler filled with my mother's tuna sandwiches and brownies. We baby-sat for our cousins and learned to feed and diaper a baby and to handle the terrible twos. We spent the summers at the city beach with Great-Aunt Lena and Cousin Marie and her kids, listening to the women gossip about the family and having races to the float with our cousins.

The highlight of a week of school and cleaning was often a visit by grandmother and a maiden aunt for tea. If Grandma's turquoise 1963 Skylark was parked next to the hedge, I knew the damask cloth was on the dining room table and my mother's ironstone teapot was waiting to be filled as soon as we walked in the door. Tea was poured into real tea cups, with saucers even, for my little sisters, and homemade Italian cookies were served. It was a real treat if my uncle's pretty, young wife stopped by with the baby, and we'd take turns holding the baby and playing with her. Grandma would give us each a dollar and show us her latest gadget, such as the miniature silver box that opened to reveal a small pad and silver pencil with which to keep track of canasta scores.

I loved to spend time at Grandma's house as the only child in a household of adoring women. If Grandma was busy waxing the kitchen floor, Aunt Anita could be counted on to make a wedding dress for a Barbie, complete with hand-sewn seed pearls. She was our favorite aunt, a great baker, and the only person I ever knew who made her own potato chips.

Aunt Anita worked at "the shop," a small garment factory run by my old family friends. When we picked her up after work, I would beg to be allowed to enter the noisy, low-slung building in the heart of the Italian neighborhood, where the smell of pressed cotton and the roar of the sewing machines overwhelmed me as I walked through the door. Tall barrels of fabric remnants stood next to cutting tables, and I was allowed to rummage through the bins, selecting cuts of colorful prints to make into doll clothes. The closing bell rang at four o'clock each day, cutting off the electricity to the long rows of sewing machine tables that ran the lengths of the main room. For a few seconds, the deafening racket would be replaced with a roaring silence before the machine operators, all women, stood up and collected their lunch thermoses and street shoes and prepared to go home. Some knew me, some not. But they all had the familiar look of the large nose and broad features of my female relatives, and all smiled at the sight of Anita's niece patiently waiting beside the car for her aunt to appear.

I did not know what a sweatshop was nor had I ever heard the term used in those days, but I knew that my aunt's back was never the same after years of bending over the needle. To me, the shop was just an exotic and mysterious place. To this day, the smell of pressed cotton floods me with memories of the shop, which is probably the source of my own love of fabric and textiles.

○ ○ ○

As simple as our family lives were, there were emotional undercurrents that surfaced frequently. With five girls and little money, my mother juggled chores and babies and devised charts to determine whose night it was to do the dishes and whose turn it was to wash her hair. Our young female minds were more engaged in the sisterly fairness of the telephone rota, the shared box of Modess pads in the linen closet, and the much-coveted single bedroom than in study of the catechism.

The smell of Aqua Net and Dippity Do mingled with the acrid smell of Lysol and Mr. Clean as we took turns washing the one bathroom on Saturday mornings. Bobby pins and pink curlers were traded like currency on Saturday nights. Items of clothing that had been "borrowed" without permission were retrieved on raids through the offender's bedroom with as much aggression as the war in Vietnam.

My parents tried to maintain order in this maelstrom of feminine *strum* and *drang*, but they were both overwhelmed with the chores and the bills and the needs of five daughters. They disciplined with a raise in their voice and a smack in their hand. A typical post-war Dad, my father was at work most of the time and participated only in major events, such as teaching us how to drive. But he did not involve himself in the nitty-gritty of our upbringing. As long as we were respectful, clean, and ready for nine o'clock Sunday mass, he was free to retreat after dinner behind the newspaper and a cloud of pipe smoke as we bickered over whose turn it was to clear the table. The men in the family were loved, honored, and respectfully feared. But we all knew that they held only cameo roles in our family's largely female cast.

True decision-making and discipline were wielded by my mother, who often showed the strain of juggling many children on a small budget with little help. My mother was as much a daughter of her own strong mother as she was a mother herself. She did her best to straddle the matriarchal world of her mother's and the contemporary worlds of her daughters. I vividly recall my mother hanging wet sheets in the basement on clotheslines my father had strung while arguing with my oldest sister, Carol, about her wanting to move out into an apartment with friends in the city. I remember my mother crying after my sister slammed out of the house because my mother refused to give her permission to move out, something that "good girls" from "good families" just did not do.

The turbulence of the sixties was cracking the rigid mold of family life. The world was exploding around us. Peace demonstrations and race problems were common at the public high school I attended. My friends were getting high with their teachers, and being a virgin was a disgrace. My parents were unapproachable on these matters and preferred not to know our involvement. It was up to the sisters to police ourselves, to act as moral barometers for each other, allowing a certain amount of outrageous conduct but not enough to cross the line that would bring it to the attention of our parents. We left behind our childhood animosities and began our own ritual of tea when we all got home from school and work, gathered around the kitchen table, griping about our courses, our jobs, our parents.

At college I learned to excel in academics to distinguish myself. I was exposed to brilliant female professors who lived single, scholarly lives in Manhattan and spent hours in their offices preparing for our courses. I became a resident assistant and held the heads of drunken freshman girls as they wretched after their first beer binge. I covered for friends whose families called when they were sleeping in their boyfriends' rooms. I drove my best friend for an abortion and watched her that night for signs of hemorrhaging while I finished my Latin homework.

I was caught up in the rise of feminism and soon began to question all the feminine images I was raised with. When I went home to visit, I denounced the birthday cake roses, the handmade Barbie doll clothes, and what I saw as the enslavement of women's lives for the good of the family. My aunts and grandmother listened tolerantly, usually with an bemused expression on their faces, and said, "Good for you, make something of yourself." I was always disappointed at their low-key reactions to my speeches.

I straddled two feminine worlds: the intellectual, feminist archetype where I wanted to go to law school, and the domestic, feminine world of my family where I was expected to live at home until I married and quit work when the babies came. I was presented with two disparate female icons and refused to devote myself to either at the sacrifice of the other.

Eventually, I became a prosecutor and also was the first of my friends to marry and the first of my sisters to have a child, a daughter, Jessica. As the end of my maternity leave grew near, I knew I would not return to work. I could not wrench myself from my baby daughter's newborn smell or tolerate the thought of someone else's hands pushing her stroller on walks. My colleagues were aghast that I would quit such a prestigious and hard-won position, but they were relieved when I announced my plans to start a law practice from home. My family, on the other hand, was delighted when I quit but aghast when I announced my intentions to practice. I ignored them all, and with much trepidation, settled in to raise our daughter and build a practice.

The first winter after the baby was born was long and hard: housebound with a crying infant, forty-five miles away from my family, with a husband who left before sun up and returned home after dark. I couldn't even use the phone very much because we were on such a tight budget, and I didn't know a soul to invite in for a cup of tea. Often the only sound I heard besides the cries of the baby was the plow scraping the snow off the road.

With the first hint of spring and promise of clear roads, I secured the baby in her car seat and drove home. Everyone had promised to be at my mother's that day. The dining room table was set for tea, and my Aunt had made her Italian cookies. Great Aunt Gussie and my uncles' young wives were there also, waiting for me to arrive with the baby. I walked in and saw these women gathered around the dining room table drinking from the same china floral tea cups we had used all these years and immediately felt as though I were a youngster again coming in from school.

The baby slept most of the afternoon, but we were still sitting around the tea table when she cried. I brought her downstairs, shy again at my new-found status as mother. I held the baby up and handed her over the table to my grandmother who made soft cooing noises at her first great-grandchild. Our hands touched briefly over the table as I gave the baby to her, and I felt the passing of the generations in her hands. My status suddenly changed. I was no longer the baby-sitter cousin or little sister or the obedient daughter.

I was the mother, the progenitor, and I had come home to sit at my rightful place at the table of the feminine. At the tea table, I finally merged the two disparate icons into a new, unique being of woman that was me. I raised my daughter in benediction, offering her to the family like the host held high at Sunday Mass, consecrating her to the table of family, blessing her over the teacups, the fifth generation of women at table.

I live a thousand miles away from my family now. I still talk almost daily with my sister and my mother, catching up on the antics of our children and the needs of our aging relatives. We see each other for long weeks in the summer, and my mother spends a few weeks with us at the holidays. I have a wide circle of female friends, and I belong to several spiritual groups of women who discuss books like *Circle of Stones*. Still, I have to settle for the figure of Bella Nonna tacked up on my study wall, smiling down at me, her teapot always full, her cup running over.

Loretta Benedetto Marvel is a writer who is working on her first novel and has had short stories published. She has been happily married for twenty-one years and has three children. She has moved back to her hometown and once again is enjoying sitting around the tea table with her mother, sisters, and extended family.

Hands
by Meredith Haines
Alexandria, Virginia

These square palms
stubby fingers
wide fingernails
wrinkled knuckles
Oh how I hate them.

If I believed
I would pray
for feminine hands
long skinny fingers
perfectly manicured fingernails
skin as smooth and white as
milk.

Hands that are too good
to catch you tripping on dust
nibbling your nails
grabbing bark
counting coins
finishing strong after a 50 fly
catching frogs by the lake.

I wonder what it's like
to be pristine.

My mother wonders too
for these are her
mother's hands
and hers
and mine.

Meredith Haines recently became the proud bearer of a brand-new bachelor's degree from the University of Virginia. While getting her feet wet in the real world, she harbors dreams of much bigger and better adventures. Though only an occasional poet, she works hard to surround herself with people she admires, hoping some inspiration will rub off. She still lives close to her parents, who over the years have been her brave supporters and her biggest heroes.

Unseen Hands
by Seema K. Singh, M.D.
Rochester, New York

*W*hen I reflect upon the women who have supported and guided me, I envision a pair of hands aged with wisdom, gently but firmly molding a clay pot as it spins rapidly on the potter's wheel.

I see my maternal grandmother, dressed in traditional Punjabi clothing, a scarf draped over her head, seated in front of the fire, cooking a traditional meal of chapati and vegetables for my brother and me, caring for us while my mom was at work. I imagine how she must have weathered life as a widow with six children to raise, of which three were daughters.

"Laxmi, why do you waste money educating these girls of yours? Save the money for their dowry." Such were the voices of advice that surrounded my grandmother. Voices of other women who could not understand why my grandmother, who herself had barely completed an elementary school education, insisted that all of her three daughters be working, with stable careers before their marriage.

I recall my mom telling me of the day when we were to leave India to join my dad in New York. My mom was weeping silently, holding my younger toddler brother in her arms, as I stood clutching the fold of her saree.

"But I won't know anyone there, Mataji, and you won't be there," my mom cried.

"Don't be silly. Your place is with your children and husband. And take this." My grandmother handed my mom her yellowed, weathered version of the Bhagavad-Gita. "Whenever you feel alone, sit and pray and read this. Just take your children in your lap and read this. You will be comforted."

My thoughts turn to a more tragic day. Shots ring in the air. Ambulance sirens screech through the sky. A telephone ringing cuts across the thick summer afternoon siesta. Papa has been shot. My mom's voice is strangely calm over the phone. "Come with your brother to the hospital. Come right away. Come . . ." And then there is only sobbing.

The moments and days and weeks that follow are etched permanently in my mind. The hospital corridors filled with sterile disinfectant. The white coats of the doctors and the greens scrubs of the surgeons. The blinking lights of the ICU. The machinery hum of the ventilators. The hospital cafeteria, where I could smell only the disinfectant.

One image will always be dear to me: my mother, sitting in the chapel, dressed in traditional Punjabi clothing, with a red scarf draped over her head, praying almost ceaselessly, often sleeplessly for my papa's life. In her stance the story from Indian mythology is revived. In my mom is Savitri, who brings back her husband even from Yama, the Lord of Death himself.

As I wait for the water to brew for my husband's tea . . . as I knead the dough to make chapati . . . as I add the turmeric and coriander and cumin from my spice box to the vegetables on the stove . . . as I sit in prayer reciting scriptures in Hindi and Sanskrit . . . as I study yoga and meditation and attempt to teach this to my fellow medical colleagues, I feel the presence of my mother and my grandmother and her mother and those before her. I am not alone.

I am supported and guided, held up by unseen hands.

Seema Khaneja Singh, M.D., is a pediatrician and yoga teacher who lives in Rochester, New York, with her physician husband. Originally from India, she is inspired by the ancient Vedic way of life, which she hopes to share through her writings and work. She recently completed a year as a fellow in general pediatrics at the University of Rochester and is now pursuing further studies in homeopathy.

The Grandmother Tree
by Chris Rummer
Clifton, Preston, United Kingdom

W hen I was a child, I loved to go to my grandmother's apartment in Queens, New York. She lived in a lovely, old brick building that my child's eye likened to a castle, with a rounded tower and red, wooden door. Across from her apartment was the parish house for the Episcopal Church, with a large front yard in which stood a big, old oak tree. I would sit in the rocking chair in the little front room my grandmother called a "sun porch," rocking and gazing up at that big, old tree. How majestic it was! How gnarled its roots, as its branches seemed to touch the sky. I could lose myself in those branches, traveling upward, free as a bird, or marveling at the massive spread of its roots, holding it firmly in the earth. As I rocked in that quiet space, I could hear the church bells ring each quarter of an hour, and yet, it was as if time stood still. As if that place, that time when I felt safe in the quiet of my grandmother's house, was all there was.

Many years later, as I was leading a group of teachers through a guided imagery, I saw my grandmother's oak tree in my mind's eye. This time, the tree had a door, and when I entered, there were stairs that lead up and down at the same time. Stairs taking me to both the heavens above and the depths of the earth below. Steps that carried me forward to my own grandmother years yet to come. Suddenly, I was in a time beyond time, a crone, one who embraced all things, both light and dark, laughing at death, embracing life, at home with the absurd, the paradoxical.

Now, behind my house in a small village in England, there is a churchyard filled with big, old trees, shading the graves of some who died long before my native country was born. The church bells ring, and time stands still, as the gnarled roots reach down into Mother Earth and the branches point to Heaven.

Since leaving her psychology practise in Washington and moving to England in 1997, Dr. Rummer has been leading workshops on leadership and coming of age for adolescent girls and the professionals who work with them, as well as workshops on cross-cultural change. She is currently writing a novel about a young American girl who goes back in time to meet her great-great-great-great grandmother in Wales.

Section 2

Woman to Woman:
Individual Women
Who Made a Difference

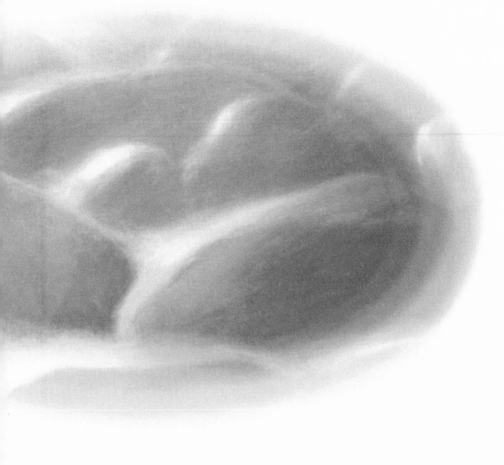

Mrs. Brown's Tears
by Linda C. Wisniewski
Doylestown, Pennsylvania

She was crying when she told us.
She was very tall, with short, wiry, light-brown hair, and she always wore a suit or a skirt and blouse. She was very smart and often funny. She clearly loved to teach. When she strode down the long halls, her stacked heels made a loud noise on the wooden floor. I don't know how old she was, nor did I care back then. In my memory, she looks about thirty-five. It was October 1960, and John F. Kennedy was running for president of the United States. In our junior high school, there were no computers, no air-conditioning, no Nikes, and no women wearing pants. Although I would not hear about women's liberation for a few more years, Mrs. Brown was about to teach me something about freedom.

On that sunny October morning, I was fourteen years old. Looking at my future barreling down at me like a runaway train, I was as scared as the proverbial deer in the headlights. Where would I go, what would I do, who would I be?

For years, I had been dreaming about the day when I would leave home to live my life. I knew I would have to leave, and travel far. Remaining near my emotionally needy parents would prevent me from ever finding a life of my own. Dad was abusive, and Mom was his victim. Both of them dashed my dreams and discouraged my ideas for my life. They were afraid for me and for themselves. Afraid for me, because seeking a life different from theirs was, to their minds, too risky and fraught with dangerous possibilities. Afraid for themselves, because my dreams seemed like a rejection of their own choices, which would leave them alone together one day.

At our house the routine was repeated every few days. Dad yelled and cursed, Mom cried, and everything stayed the same, both of them unhappy and afraid. My sister and I tried very hard not to cry because that would mean that Dad had "won," beaten us at the crazy game our family played. In my experience when women cried, they lost; the game was over. They "broke down" and went quietly away.

When I was growing up, it was important to cover up the hurt Dad was causing, even to the point of denying that it was wrong. My sister and I were actually ashamed, as if we had somehow deserved it. Mom would tell us that it was "not so bad . . . at least he doesn't get drunk, or gamble, like some men do, or hit us." We learned that we were somehow inadequate because we cried.

I was such a quiet child that my mother and aunts worried about me. I never spoke in class. When we went to church, I sat in the pew like a porcelain statue. I was afraid of everything, but especially of doing or saying the wrong thing, so I did not move or speak.

Then, on an autumn day in ninth grade civics class, Mrs. Brown shook my world.

Mrs. Brown's voice was always loud, but suddenly it was shaking and had a higher pitch. Tears shone in her large brown eyes. "I am very angry today because we have been denied permission to go to the John Kennedy rally. This is a once-in-a-lifetime event that will be happening a few blocks away from our school, yet you will not be allowed to go and watch American history as it is taking place."

She stopped to take a breath, and went on.

"Our principal, Mr. Werner, feels that this is a partisan event that we cannot attend. We would appear to be endorsing Kennedy for president of the United States. I promised to take you to see Richard Nixon, if he comes to town, but Mr. Werner will not allow that either."

She paused for another deep breath. When she resumed, her voice was even shakier.

"I am sorry because I wanted you to have this experience. And I am very, very angry at Mr. Werner."

The entire class fell silent. We were stunned by our teacher's anger. We were shocked that she had stood up to her boss. We were thrilled that she cared enough about us to fight for our big chance to witness history. We were especially proud that she was treating us like grownups by explaining exactly how she felt. For me, however, it was much more than that. For the first time, I saw a strong woman who was not afraid to cry angry tears, and my world opened up like a flower.

Mrs. Brown refused to behave like an acquiescent female. She did not sugar coat the truth. She was clearly angry and frustrated with Mr. Werner and told us exactly why this was so. She spoke through her tears and was not defeated by them, and I had never seen anything like it.

Years later, I thought of her as I cried in angry frustration. The agency I worked for had been running an essay contest, and I was the agency's spokesperson. The topic was hiring the handicapped, and the winning essay had some negative things to say about a very large local company, which also happened to be a major sponsor of the contest. Their representative wanted the winning essay disqualified because it was "not accurate." Since the essay was to be published in the local newspaper, it would be terrible publicity. I understood his dilemma, but a small seed of courage had been planted in my heart by Mrs. Brown, and it was about to flower.

Deciding that I would refuse to disqualify the winning essay, I was shaking and scared. I knew that I might cry when I confronted my boss in his office.

"Linda, please sit down. I have never seen you so upset!" Mr. Burnside exclaimed.

"Of course, I am upset, " I said, through angry tears. "You are asking me to be dishonest, and cover up the truth because someone is embarrassed by it."

I lived through that moment, and got to keep my job and my self-respect, even though the controversial essay was disqualified by another member of the committee.

Over the years, I continued to speak up in scary situations, often through angry tears. Many times, people such as Mr. Burnside wanted to talk about my tears to avoid the issue I was angry about. In time, however, my self-confidence grew as I learned to speak my mind.

The toughest confrontation, however, involved my own father. I had just turned fifty, and that runaway train was coming at me again. This time what had me paralyzed was the knowledge that my time for speaking the truth was limited. Everything I did took on an added sense of urgency, until finally one day as I listened to my father once again call my mother, "Stupid," and no one protested, I knew I had to act.

I told him I wanted to talk about something that had been bothering me for a long time. I said that when he called my mother names, I felt sick to my stomach. Quickly and angrily, he interrupted.

"You don't know what you're talkin' about. You sound like you been drinkin'."

My heart ached and pounded in my chest. My hands were shaking and my eyes filled. I continued through my tears, explaining how I felt, until my Dad walked away from me.

My little boy was in the room, silently listening. He came to me and climbed into my lap.

That night, I caressed my legs as I smoothed on lotion and marveled at the unfamiliar love I felt for myself.

Of course, speaking up through your tears does not guarantee the outcome you desire. On that autumn day in 1960, Mrs. Brown didn't get what she wanted. Our class did not get to see John F. Kennedy. I didn't get everything I wanted from Mr. Burnside; the contest was still rigged in favor of the corporate sponsor. My dad did not stop abusing my mom.

But sometimes you get something you did not know to ask for, something even more valuable than the need of the moment.

By learning to speak through my fear, I got my self-respect. My son got a lesson from watching his mom that anger salted with tears is perfectly okay. And Mrs. Brown gets to live forever in the heart of a little girl who grew up to write about her for anyone to read as long as the story can be told.

It has never been easy for me to speak through my tears, but when I need courage, I like to think of her, standing tall in front of our class. Then, in my heart, it is October 1960 again, and the world is filled with possibilities.

Linda C. Wisniewski is a librarian who lives with her family in Bucks County, Pennsylvania. A late bloomer, she went to her first protest march at thirty-eight, had her second child at forty-three, started her own business at forty-four, and published her first article at fifty. She is working on a book of essays about her life with scoliosis. Linda is an active member of the International Women's Writing Guild, and the Story Circle Network, where she facilitates an on-line group for women who are ready to tell their own stories.

The Women of My Life
by D-L Nelson
LeGrand-Saconnex, Switzerland

Clara

My daughter is thirty. I tell people
we've had twenty-eight wonderful years.
Five and thirteen are best forgotten.
She was always independent,
insisting
on holding her own bottle
insisting
on making her own decisions
which were almost always right
and certainly as good as mine.
She is nothing like me.
I am neat,
needing things in neurotic order.
She marks her territory
scattering her possessions
wherever she goes.
She is good at math and
can put furniture together.
I am good at words and
can put furniture together, but wrong
so she fixes it.
We lived in a small flat for nine months,
agreeing that our relationship
was more important than neat or messy,
making a lie of the saying two women
can't get along under the same roof.

*S*usan

She knows if I'm well

by the way I walk through a room.

Maybe

because we have walked in each other's souls.

She saved my daughter's life

and thus saved mine.

When we had a rough patch,

I thought she was reading my journal.

so I wrote in green ink,

      "Susan, I know you're reading this."

In blue ink, the next day I found,

      "No I'm not, just keep writing."

A problem with old friends

is they don't let you fool yourself.

It works both ways.

Each year we go on retreat,

one year in Argeles-sur-mer,

the next in Ocean Grove,

walk on the beach,

eat fresh corn,

lick ice cream cones,

listen to music,

rent movies,

read to each other,

play Scrabble,

talk about men, my writing,

her teaching, women's studies,

politics, history, and art—

freed from chores

it is a renewal of all

that is good in our lives.

Mardy

A boy with beautiful blue eyes
dated Mardy and me at the same time.
At sixteen we decided
we liked each other better than him.
Tied by the telephone cord for hours,
we told our dreams.

When I was getting divorced,
Mardy held the glue pot
as I pieced myself together.
When we walked in the woods behind
her folks' Maine cabin, we tasted wild
blackberries as she spoke
of nightmares.

And now that we are happy,
She tells me we are not just
foul-weather friends.

Norma

My father fell in love with my step-mom
when they were both married to other people.
She swirled across the dance floor in a
white gown embroidered with violets
and into his arms.
They never had his children or her children.
"We have our children," she always said in
a tone that let everyone know
there was no alternative.

When she visits,
we play cards.
She wipes me out,
no dainty widow lady, she.
We go to restaurants,
laugh a lot,
share memories of my Dad
and build new ones of our own.

Lillian
They met in secretarial school,
Lillian and my mother.
Agreed on nothing for sixty years,
stayed friends and fought
over every issue.
At eighty Lillian
picketed the British consulate,
marched for pro choice
and told of a man in an
Irish pub who raved about her hair,
suggesting they sleep together.
      "Did you?" I asked.
She shook her head.
"I was wearing a wig.
I didn't want him to know."
      "And if you weren't?"
She just smiled.

ar

No one, least of all me, knows why I
called my grandmother "Dar," but soon
the world followed, even her friends
from childhood. She never minded being
renamed in her fifties.
When she baked a cake, she used
all the batter, but gave me the spoon to lick.
She read me *The Bobbsey Twins* and made
mudpies that looked good enough to eat.
A high school drop out
she prodded me through algebra,
tested my Latin verbs,
knew more history than
the substitute teacher.
Despite her thick glasses,
she told me I was beautiful.
She was a New England Yankee.
Right was right.
Wrong was wrong.
When she had eye surgery,
she didn't tell the doctor
the anesthesia hadn't worked,
thinking it *should* hurt.
And when she lost two children
she bore that hurt too.

Dar saw five wars,
Lillian only four.
Norma was a WAVE in
World War II
while, Mardy, Susan and I

can touch names on a
long black wall in D.C.
Names of boys we played with
who will play no more. Llara?
She knows war as a media event,
as men with mikes talk on CNN.
These women's lives span
the inventions of electricity to e-mail.
Dar abandoned her horse and buggy,
was called The Woman with the Ford
while the rest of us jump on
planes to change continents at whim.

◌ ◌ ◌

No Stantons,
Steinems,
Sangers,
or Curies
in this group.
They march by history,
not make it.
No one will write books,
sing songs,
make movies,
or sculpt statues for public places
honoring their lives.
They honor themselves.

*D-L Nelson's writing has appeared in six countries and has been read on BBC World
Radio. Writing poetry is so new, she doesn't yet consider herself a poet, but a "po." She
hopes to find a publisher for her five novels, three of which have won literary awards. She
has a M.A. Creative Writing from Glamorgan University, Wales. Originally a New
England Yankee, she lives in Geneva, Switzerland, and is the overseas correspondent for
Credit Union Times.*

Things of the Heart
by Janet L. Doane
Santa Rosa, California

*I*t's my altar really, the shelf in the kitchen, displaying all things of the heart. Rose's photographs are tucked along every corner: the sunset aflame with golden rays backlighting a dramatic cloud, the tropical flowers from Sufrie. Rose's gift of moon candles, a color for every phase of the moon's cycles, sits complete in a glass crystal holder. Then there is the fine china teapot she and Jane sent for my birthday, its glaze a pattern of purple and blue flowers, graced with a single matching teacup.

I remember the day the box arrived. When I saw the teapot, it felt like a Grandmother's teapot—the grandmother I will one day become. I could hear the grandchildren saying, "I want to drink from Grandma's teacup . . . No, *I* do. You got to last time . . . *Grandma!*"

The teapot arrived in September after my husband and I had spent my fiftieth birthday on Mt. Shasta—an appropriate place to contemplate the seasons of one's life. The day before returning, we had stopped at the Shasta Herb Store to stock up on tinctures. I was planning to start drinking more tea, to keep a hot brew in the studio while the paint flew onto the paper.

How did my friends know? It was a deep sorrow and joy, coming home, receiving that teapot. Five months have already passed, and I have yet to make tea in it, as much as I want to. I think I'm waiting for Rose.

Now I'm packing up the house to move again, just as I packed the house two years ago to move from Connecticut to Sonoma—when I said goodbye to Rose, when the tight grip of our hands imprinted deep within our hearts. I can still see her radiant smile, hear her laughing, and remember her deep, brown eyes—eyes that knew me, eyes that I was never afraid to be held in.

Today I pack—the teapot, the cup, Rose's photos, one by one, not knowing where I will be next month. The uncertainty is unsettling. We will travel, Rose and I together, despite the distance. She with my poems, writing, and paintings, and I with her photographs of orchids from St. Lucia and of sunsets of streaming, golden light.

I will wait to pour hot tea until we are both together again. And we will drink the goodness from the one cup, taking turns to sip and swallow, sigh and remember.

○ ○ ○

A NOTE FROM THE AUTHOR: When I moved with my husband from Connecticut to California in 1996, I grieved for my friend Rose. She and Jane had been part of a remarkable core group of women that were the glue that held me together, along with a husband with a heart of gold, as I journeyed through the pain of uncovering early childhood trauma, coupled with the upheaval of the onset of menopause.

We maintained our relationship with phone calls and cards. Rose often sent beautiful photocards of images she'd taken during family trips to tropical paradises, such as Barbados or Grand Cayman. I began writing poems that captured my impressions about each image. If I couldn't have Rose with me physically, at least I could feel her presence by working deeply with her photos.

The next year I joined a weekly writers group. One January night during a freewriting session, "Things of the Heart" fell onto the page. Months later an unexpected phone call came from Rose. "Guess what! I can come out! Would July be okay?"

I was stunned. After nearly three years, we would finally be together again. The anticipation and excitement of our reunion was a gift in itself. I waited for the perfect moment before I shared my story with her, reading it out loud, barely able to speak, for we were both choked with tears. As we sipped ginger tea from the single teacup, drinking from it for the first time, Rose told me she had secretly photographed the teapot. We knew our friendship had come full circle and would continue.

Janet L. Doane aspires to bring the spiritual elements in life—experiences and events that reveal the presence of God's love—into an artform where the viewer can recognize their meaning. Her vision is expressed through writing, poetry, painting, photography, and cooking, and in deep communication with family and friends. She is the author and illustrator of Almond Essence—Recipes for Making and Using Almond Nut Milk. *She and her husband currently reside in Santa Rosa, California.*

"Janet's Teapot"
Photograph by Rosemary DeLucco-Alpert
Guilford, Connecticut

Rosemary DeLucco-Alpert is a photographer living in Guilford, Connecticut, with her husband and two children. Her photographic journey began when she was a little girl and has lead her to many interesting people and places. She studied with Ansel Adams and Ruth Bernard, worked in Los Angeles as a photo editor, traveled throughout the Southwest and Caribbean, and started her own greeting card line from her photo collection. Her photographs capture beauty and simplicity, allowing the inner light of the subject to be expressed.

Circles Of Women: Within, Without, With All
by Sandy Sherman, OSU
Toledo, Ohio

On the morning of December 20, 1983, I attended Mass in the parish where I was then teaching. Having just asked to take my final vows, I heard with joy the words of that day's annual pre-Christmas gospel: "Be it done to me according to your word" (Luke 1:38).

Ten hours later, as a stranger was raping me in my classroom, I felt that God's word had somehow turned on me.

I did make my final vows but was unsure that my vow of chastity was valid. Two years later I began the round of three therapists before finding one who validated my story. The pain of the invalidation was worse than the rape itself. It was then that I made the vow that I would never *not* believe any woman's story.

The third therapist was my first experience of visitation. Just as Elizabeth, pregnant like Mary, midwifed her through her uncertainties, my therapist, violated like me, midwifed me through my pain. To the vow I had made to believe other women, I added the desire to walk with them.

One very early morning while praying, I heard a woman scream. Thinking someone was being attacked on the street, I ran to the front door to be greeted only by the silence. I gradually came to realize that the scream had come from within me.

While my therapist helped me to trust releasing the scream, my spiritual director helped me to identify the God whose voice it expressed, a God who spoke to me through music, ritual, and dance. Dancing alone was my private prayer—a vertical connection to the something I was trying to attain. But when I began to dance with others, I found the connection, which made complete my prayer, and the cross, which I understood because I had stood under it. I had long known the source of the scream; now I knew its destination.

Six years ago I found out about a program called SSSS (Sister Survivor Support Services). Knowing myself to be the only woman in my community public about my survival, I knew I needed other support even to get approval to take the training. I approached the Vicar for Religious of our diocese and found out that the local Leadership Council of Women Religious (LCWR) had recently approached her about the need for such a program. And so I followed the scream and the voice to California and came back a trained SSSS facilitator.

Every two weeks for two years, other women religious survivors and myself have gathered to share our stories. Together we recall, retell, reclaim, reconcile, and re-member our past to our present. Our stories of survival and courage are transformed into gifts for one another. While our group is small, we have come further together than any of us could have come alone. Two springs ago, when we hosted a weekend retreat, several others came out of silence to join us. The retreat has become an annual event. When screams of loneliness unite with others, they create a harmony that invites at-one-ment.

The wisdom of our circle enables me to transform my inner scream into an outer voice, which never turns women away . . . and never *not* believes them.

From the time she was a little girl, Sandy Sherman, OSU, loved to write. She is also a sacred dancer, and what she shares comes from the movement deep within her. As her spiritual director names it, it is her "ministry of word." At age forty-six, she has only recently been published in Christianity and the Arts *(November 1998),* Sisters Today *(May 2000),* Giving Voice *(Spring 2001), and is currently a new writer of movement and ritual for Network for Women's Spirituality. Sandy is currently vocation director for her community, the Toledo Ursuline Sisters.*

A Gift Gone 'Round
by June Woodall
South Hill, Virginia

*S*he calls softly my name
with the breath of ancient whispers
and the quiet strength of holiness,
the hands of the old black woman

          beckon me

to share a seat by her window
to feel time fall away
and all sense of purpose
left on the front porch,
waiting for its company.
Patience comes through the back door
and finds her seat by the window,
joining us to complete the circle
and the darkness of the woman

          glows

in the light of the morning sun
and my heart's rhythm slows
to the pace of sunlight
and the dark woman
and the warm touch of patience

          holding my hand

while time and purpose
play stickball in the yard.

June Woodall has been a physical therapist for the past twenty-three years at Community Memorial Healthcenter in South Hill, Virginia. A life-long resident of Southside, Virginia, she and her husband of twenty-two years have two teenage sons. June serves as chair of the local literacy organization, LEARN! She has been writing seriously for the past eight years.

A Little Girl's Precious Toy
by Peggy J. Simms
Alpharetta, Georgia

I had never heard the name before—Toy. How it attracted me! It seemed to me that the name represented joy and playfulness, for were not toys imminently accessible to children and created for the specific purpose of bringing joy to their hearts? Toy was mine and I was hers. I honored Toy in one of the most significant ways a little girl can honor an adult: I named my favorite doll after her.

I can see Toy and me standing outside the old car shed, known as a garage, as we begin our walk down the winding country lane. In my mind's eye I hear myself asking her about flying saucers and people from other planets. She looks straight into my eyes as I talk and listens intently. She never invalidates my questions or discounts the importance of them. She shares my curiosity and tells me what she knows about the subjects. She encourages me to learn more. She is accessible to me in ways my own parents cannot be. Years later the gift of Toy echoes in my mind and heart, as one of my stepchildren tells me, "The thing I like most about you, Peggy, is you always look right at me when I'm talking to you!"

I awaited visits to Toy's house with anticipation, knowing I would find feasts for my hungry mind and imagination; even the journey there was filled with delight. She lived in a wonderful bungalow-style home on a winding country road, just past the house where Northwest territory explorer Meriwether Lewis was born. When I walked on Toy's property, I could dream about Lewis and his exploration of foreign territory. I could bravely imagine myself having adventures and exploring new territory. I felt safe.

Inside Toy's home was an abundance of paintings, comfortable furniture, and a magnificent organ. Waiting oils, canvases, and easels stood ready for Toy's touch when her Muse provided inspiration to capture a particular scene or person with paints. I often found her engaged in a work-in-progress. She painted the familiar scenes of my life: our old farmhouse surrounded by its tall stately maples; me in my red pajamas hugging our beloved collie, Laddie Boy; and me as a teenager dressed for Cotillion. When Toy painted, it seemed so effortless. Her paintings emerged on the canvas, soft, friendly, and inviting you to enjoy the scene or get acquainted with the people or animals pictured there.

Years later, around the age of forty, I felt an inner call to paint. I was mystified by my burning desire and startled by my boldness in registering for a watercolor class, having no previous painting experience. Soon, I found an old box of watercolors, long hidden away, that I had used as a child. The red paint tray was almost empty, further identifying it as mine. Slowly other memories emerged of the child, Peggy, sitting at her desk in the corner of the living room and painstakingly drawing one of her favorite local homes, Monticello, the home of Thomas Jefferson. Every time I walk through my living room today, I see her painting of the old farmhouse where I grew up, hanging there on the wall, reminding me of the good times. When I see the small painting in my home office of Laddie and me, I recall the innocence of a little girl and her love for her precious furry playmate. I sing a song of gratitude for Toy.

Toy reminds me of one of those Russian nesting dolls, with many figures nested within one another. For me, Toy represented the fullness of being: independence and relationship, action and reflection, nullifier and creator, reason and emotion. Although she was married and had three grown children, I do not remember ever meeting her husband during all of the years I knew her. His job called him to live away from her, in the Valley. How Toy reached this arrangement with her husband and what allowed them to live this lifestyle during a time when it was obligatory for the wife to be the satellite revolving around her husband's career is still a mystery to me. Toy lived independently, cozily, and creatively.

These memories call to mind the ancient and original definition of the word "virgin," that is, dependent on no man, a self-contained being. When I first met Toy in the 1950s and forever after, as long as I knew her, she kept to this lifestyle.

When I remarried, I decided to keep my maiden name. For the first time, in a marital relationship, I kept myself intact, preserving my unique "Peggy-ness." As I write today, I wonder if I may thank Toy for yet another gift that has come to me late in life: my true virginity.

Peggy J. Simms, LCSW, is a clinical social worker, lover of people, animals, and nature, native Virginian, and Georgia transplant for the past twenty-five years. She is at work and at play on a book to re-member the Divine Feminine and how Her absence from the image of God has impacted us. She also re-members "herstory" by leading women's groups and writing about women who touched her life in meaningful ways.

Friendship Beads
by *Shelley Tracey*
County Antrim, Northern Ireland

Over and over again I realise the full depth and breadth of the friendship of women, the warmth and love and companionship and connection. I carry within me a set of friendship beads, which I have strung together from the gifts of the past and the present. Each bead is beautiful and unique and comforting, and I can find precisely the one I need at any time.

The Heather bead is strong and warm to the touch, lit right from the centre with a golden glow.

The Sandy bead is small and bright, full of vitality, its edges smooth with suffering and humour.

The most delicate transparent bead, tinged with lilac, bears Anna's gentle sweetness.

The Jane bead is jade green and star shaped, and fits right into the centre of my palm. It is always there to be found.

The Amanda bead is amber, with an intense light, reflecting passion, fierce intelligence, strong anger, love and laughter.

The Janie bead is fragile, soft to the touch, rosepink at the core.

It has something of the beauty of the bead which I know as Beverly, elegant, fair, a classic oval.

These contrast with the Tina bead, deep purple, intense, inscrutable sometimes, yet always available for me.

The Mairead bead is large and colourful, patterned with intricate Celtic designs which shelter its vulnerable centre.

The Michele bead is scented and small and round, with a turmoil of layers of colours inside.

Again and again I turn for support to the Maranú bead, pure blue and silver, which waits patiently for me, offering me the gift of knowing myself.

I am not in touch any more with a few of the women whose images sustain me. Noreen is dead, but her tiny greenblue bead, the colour of her eyes before she went blind, will always be with me.

These are just a few of the beads that compose my soul-treasure, part of the magic circle within.

Shelley Tracey, forty-two, is a South African of Latvian descent. She now lives in Northern Ireland with her husband, three children, and a host of household pets and plants. She has been writing since she was five and has had a number of short stories and poems published. She loves art, the sea, reading, gardening, and her many women friends who support and stimulate her. "Friendship Beads" is about some of these friends.

A Baroque Sunset: In Memory of Amy Clampitt
by Susan M. Tiberghien
Bellevue, Switzerland

*A*my was teaching her first poetry workshop and longed for distraction from her jittery nerves. We talked about zinnias and sparrows, about Manhattan and Geneva. We talked about voyages, about southern France, the Italian lakes,

> ". . . Imaginary
> Italy, the never-never
> vista, framed, of Stresa
> on Lago Maggiore . . ."
> —from "The Elgin Marbles"

It was in 1984. Amy's first full-length book of poetry, *The Kingfisher*, published one year earlier when Amy turned sixty-three, had pushed her to the front ranks of American poets. *The New York Times Book Review* hailed her "as one of our most distinguished contemporary poets." She was still wondering how this had happened and more precisely how to teach a poetry workshop. "It's got to have structure, I mean poetry has to have structure, but also substance. Oh dear, we'll just have to see."

We lived through that first workshop like two cronies, she the mentor, I the follower. Afterward Amy and I wrote back and forth over the ocean. She would read what I was writing, receiving it as a gift, bestowing confidence. Soon she came for a short stay in Geneva. She fit right into our house, still filled with children. She recognized and nurtured also the mother in me.

During her visit, she met with our workshop, Women Writing in Geneva, listened to our poems and prose, and one evening she gave a reading in our home. When she shared "Babel Abroad the Hellas International Express,"

> "Border halt, an hour out of Saloniki . . .
> O for a muse of slivovitz, that fiery booze,
> to celebrate this Babel, this untranslatable
> divertimento . . ."

we were there inside the compartment, finding our way across Europe. It was the story of our lives, writers coming from different cultures, living and writing in Geneva.

Another spring time when she stopped again in Geneva, we went up into the French Alps, climbing the slopes of a not-too-steep mountain. Amy identified the wild flowers in English. I knew some of them in French, the others I had forgotten in both languages. There was a bird singing close by. Amy named the winged creature. She said it sang the same song in New England. The language didn't matter for birds.

> ". . . we drop everything to listen as a
> hermit thrush distills its fragmentary,
> hesitant, in the unbroken music . . ."
> —from "The Hermit Thrush"

That spring Amy met again with our writers' workshop. She was working on a play about Dorothy Wordsworth. She read parts of the script, taking us into the pages of Dorothy's journal, the hurried scribblings of a woman keeping house, the longings of her heart. Our longings. She now knew many of our writers personally. She remembered what we were writing, asked how we were doing, encouraged us to believe in our words.

The following year, we asked Amy to write the preface to our second collection of stories and poems. She read our manuscripts and sent back an essay on language and leaving home. "The experience of being uprooted is one that happens to us all . . . Even so I am inclined to believe that in some qualitative way the urge to leave home on the one hand, and the experience of uprooting on the other, are not the same for women as for men . . . A woman as a stranger in a strange land, a woman married to a foreigner goes back to a past so ancient as to be prehistoric. . . ."

Our visits weren't all one-sided. I met Amy often in New York City, sometimes in the apartment she shared with her lawyer-friend, Hal, sometimes for coffee in the corner café at Madison and 65th. When at the café, she'd be wearing a hat. I liked her hats, especially the deep crimson velvet one, soft, with the same color ribbon. I liked also her long skirts, the paisley scarves, the gold ring on her index finger.

Amy's last visit here was after her stay at Bellagio, where she and Hal both had Rockerfeller grants at the Villa Serbelloni.

> ". . . and busy daisies
> here called *margheritas* burgeon in
> a sun the cool spleenwort shrinks from . . ."
> —from "Matrix, Villa Serbelloni, Lake Como"

This time they came together to Geneva. We walked along the lakeside. One evening during their stay, as I was fixing supper, I heard familiar jazz music in the living room. They had found one of our old records. I went to the door to look. Amy was dancing, carefree and lighthearted, her body moving to the rhythm of Louis Armstrong.

When she won her MacArthur Foundation Award, she wrote that she remained surprised, wondering what to do now. It took me back to when she was wondering about how to teach a poetry workshop, back at Hofstra University, before she started giving workshops around the country, before she started teaching at William and Mary, at Amherst, before she was poet in residence at Smith.

Then the news arrived. "It's so like me," she wrote. "I waited longer than I should have to see the doctor . . ." That summer I returned to their apartment in Manhattan. Amy was wearing her crimson hat this time inside her home. It was the summer of 1993. She was saving her strength to finish the acknowledgements for her final book of poetry, *A Silence Opens*.

> "Now and then the smell of apples
> wrinkling in the dark wells up
> from the earth-walled storm cellar . . ."
> —from "Homeland"

In the spring she wrote that she hoped soon to get up to the house she had bought with Hal in Lenox, "a small old house with a green lawn and a rose of Sharon bush." In June an envelope postmarked Lenox arrived, containing their marriage announcement and the wedding photo. Amy's hat this time was golden, with a light pink ribbon. She was dressed in white.

Hal's shirt was deep blue.

I took the bus to Lenox in August, a few weeks before she died. Hal was waiting for me at the bus stop, sitting on the town bench. Amy, bedridden, welcomed me to their new house, describing the rooms, the old pieces of furniture she and Hal had found rummaging around yard sales and antique shops, the paintings. On the windowsill near her bed, there was a white porcelain vase with blossoms from the rose of Sharon bush in the yard, white bell-shaped flowers bordered in pink.

When she was tired from visiting, I'd sit close by at the dining table and talk with Hal. We talked about the rose of Sharon, remembering it was an Old Testament flower but not knowing the reference. "It's from the second chapter of the Song of Songs," Amy answered, listening to us from her bed. We looked up the words in her Bible: "I am a rose of Sharon, a lily of the valleys . . . He has taken me to his banquet hall, and the banner he raises over me is love."

Susan M. Tiberghien grew up in New York but has lived in Geneva, Switzerland, for over thirty years. Author of Looking for God *and* Circling to the Center, *she is grateful for the invisible web that binds us together and that brought her the opportunity to express appreciation and love to Amy Clampitt in* The Circle Continues.

For Julia
by Naomi Wahmhoff Gingerich
Goshen, Indiana

Electric woman
the first time I met you
—wild lightning—
I hid
afraid of becoming
ashes
the next time
I marveled
the third
I was drawn
as pale moth
to white hot flame
and so what
if I am ashes
to your sizzling fire
I promise
to be
live coals.

Naomi Wahmhoff Gingerich was born the ninth in a family of ten children raised in rural Michigan. She has strong connections in both Catholic and Anabaptist circles, and is bilingual in Spanish and English. Her life has taken her across many borders—geographical, cultural, and spiritual—and she writes in response to those journeys. Poetry helps her scale cliffsides, ford rivers, and build the bridges that connect her many worlds.

'Dem Bones Gonna Dance Again
by Lilith E. Hunt
Western, North Carolina

Stories—powerful and poignant—must surely lie within the tarnished antique portraits that line the walls of my home. Portraits of women from long ago hang alongside faded snapshots, all of which were framed in honor of the women I do not truly know. What lies behind, beneath, and within these frames are the unknown and the untold stories—stories rich in history, my history, stories I will never hear or know. If only I could go back to the time when the women—the sisters, the aunts, and the grandmothers—were gathered there around the baby-grand piano in that Southern sitting room. I so often wonder what their stories might have entailed. If only the portraits could speak to me now, then I would know the stories.

I would know them also if, as a child, I had had a mother who was not emotionally scarred, a mother who as a child could have reached first inside herself to learn who she was and then as a woman claimed that Self so she could honor it and help me, her only daughter, begin to find her own Self. But this did not happen. Alcoholism ravaged not only my mother's body but her soul as well. It robbed me of the opportunity to sit amongst my family circle. Yet somehow amidst all of the turbulence and loss, I received an unexpected gift.

For if you look closely at the pictures of these southern white women—Daughters of the Confederacy, even those of the American Revolution—your eye may be drawn toward one portrait that stands apart from all the others. It is of a woman, dignified, honorable, poignant in her own quiet beauty. A woman of dark skin, much unlike the others. A woman named Alma. A woman whose very name in Spanish means "soul." She was my beloved nanny for the first twelve months of my life before my family moved to another city and she could not go with us.

I do not remember exactly when Alma left, but my spirit and my body remember the devastating emptiness of that day: the day that no one came to wipe my tears, or my runny nose, the day that no one rocked me to sleep or came in the night when the tigers haunted my dreams. No one came. No parents, no sisters, no aunts, no grandmothers. No one. My image of that day is of a curly blonde-headed toddler standing in her crib, tears flowing, nose running, arms fiercely shaking the bars of the crib, her voice crying out in utter despair for someone, anyone, to come and comfort her. No person ever came.

From that day forward, I lived in isolation from my family. I learned to live on my "tiptoes," not because I was a toddler but because it was a way to remain out of "her" sight, a way to avoid the indignation, the mocking, the scorning. And, most of all, it was a way to avoid my mother's lack of recognition that I even existed. It was possible for her to go for hours, days, even weeks without speaking to me or acknowledging my existence. So I sought warmth wherever I could and from whomever I could. I found warmth at home by squeezing my body onto the narrow, thin shelves of the paneling that covered our furnace in the basement. I could lie there unnoticed, quietly soaking up the warmth of the furnace. The sadness I felt in my "comfort place" was not that I had so little warmth in my life but rather that no one realized for hours that I was even missing.

Throughout those incredibly lonely, desolate years, I had a constant image. An image of bones, my bones, my whole childish skeleton lying inside a dormer window drawer in my bedroom. It was an image that used to haunt me because I thought my bones had no flesh on them. That they were indeed dead bones. Never being told that Alma even existed until I was twenty-six years old, I had thought that no one had ever cared for me, that my bones were there in the drawer, disconnected, lifeless, without even the comfort of my favorite Winnie-the-Pooh book or a warm snuggle from my beloved stuffed rabbit, "Floppy."

One evening, while under the influence of alcohol, my mother, with anger and envy in her voice, told me about Alma and how she "pampered" me, played with me, and spoiled me rotten. I was stunned. Who was this woman of whom no words had ever before been spoken? I asked many questions, none of which were answered then. Few are answered to this day.

Learning that I had indeed, at some point in my life, had someone who loved me so very much was overwhelmingly powerful for me. It is only recently that dreams and images have begun to unfold, dreams that reveal her gifts to me. This awareness has changed both the image of myself in the crib and of my bones in the drawer. For now, as I draw these images in my women's art therapy group, this is what I am able to see:

The toddler remains in the crib, sobbing, shaking, crying out for warmth and comfort and the unconditional love that can come only from a parent's eyes. This time someone comes. She comes in the form of a great light. That light is Alma. The radiant, blinding light is literally her soul passing onward and inward to me, breathing life and hope and survival into every cell of my being.

You see, I found out that Alma was murdered by her boyfriend shortly after she left our family. I believe with all my heart that when that hideous event occurred she gave me her strength and her light. No longer is the toddler alone in the crib. There are now mermaids adorned in white and silver-sequined gowns who circle the crib, keeping harm from touching the child, allowing a new Circle of Women to approach the crib and offer their love for her. Now the light shines brightly through the window. Alma is there, and as I look out the window when the moon shines brightly, I know that once upon a time I was indeed loved.

I softly blow a goodnight kiss to my very own Grandmother Moon.

My other vivid image—of my bones lying in a lifeless fetal position there in the bedroom drawer—has changed as well. While I had previously thought of my bones there as discarded, worthless remnants of a once vivacious toddler, I am now able to envision Alma, with deep sorrow in her wounded, soulful heart searching throughout the house for the softest blanket she could find. She knew the day was at hand when we would have to part, and she knew the isolation in which I would have to survive. So she sought out a warm, thickly cushioned safe place for me to rest until the day when life would be safe enough for my bones to reconnect and dance—dance barefoot and free—upon the cool summer grass once again.

And so with her warm and loving copper-toned arms, she must have rocked me gently, singing her sweet African lullaby that my heart knew so well, holding me tightly for the last time before that moment came when she had to slowly open the drawer and gently place me there, wrapped in the blanket that held, in each of its threads, her passionate love for me. She must have truly known it was a safe place where no one would disturb me or hurt me. What a gift she gave me and what deep faith she must have had that, at some point in my life, the conditions would be just right for me to come out from the darkness into the light.

She bonded with me and I with her. We became soulmates, a beautiful blend of ebony and ivory, light and dark intertwined. While I am deeply grateful for the intertwining, as I begin to feel the light and joy she has given me, I also find myself one of many white women who owe their very lives to the love and nurture of the dark-skinned women who traveled, against their will, torn from their families, toward a life of servitude to the white men and women of America, land of oppression for both the dark-skinned and the light-skinned women. But that is changing too, ever so slowly, but changing nonetheless, as each of us, no matter what skin color we may be, begins to tell our Story. For me, I would have no Story to offer this day if it were not for my beloved Alma who has already begun to help 'dem bones dance upon the grass as they once did so very long ago.

Lilith E. Hunt is a counselor by profession and an advocate for women and youth by passion. She is currently active in developing nurturing community for herself and her family. Lilith is enjoying re-learning how to play, paint, sculpt, laugh, and yes, dance once again. She hopes to publish more writings about her journey into wholeness as her experiences unfold along the way.

Tribute
by Karen Laudenslager McDermott
Geneva, Switzerland

Lights dim, silks rustle, then settle
under cupids and crystal chandeliers.
A conductor steps to the podium,
the golden hall fades to a spot.
Fluttering at my nose, my hand ungloved
carries the faint scent of turnip or
a scrubbed potato. Through
the wavy mirror of memory
I smell other hands, pungent
cool and chapped against my forehead
brushing away tears, they float in
with the Strauss, gnarled wonders
that have picked and peeled
sliced and scraped. I finger pearls
on black velveteen, they cut fat
into flour, deftly crimp
a milk-pie crust. They pull weeds,
throw grain, crumble bread.

As the soloist sits in long blue satin
another form settles, hefty
on a needlepoint stool, a puff
of winter stew permeates her person
her sweater, her scratchy wool skirt.
She plays the piano like a demon,
apron ties swinging with enthusiasm,
those thick fingers never miss a key.

Her little feet pump the pedals and I
dance jubilant, around the table.

A sweet breathy tune sails out
over rapt quiescent faces, I sink
into a steamy bath, the ritual scrub
administered from her knees, sleeves
pushed up past fleshy elbows
sweat at her brow. These eyes are deep,
melancholy as the French horn motif
full of untold stories.

In their world, women washed and folded
dusted and polished. Ironing out
my wrinkles, they sewed me, matter-of-fact
into a grown-up gown. By the time
the heroic drums of Brahms die away
those unstoppable hands are quiet,
folded on shrunken laps.
I clap hard. Hard enough to cry.

"Tribute" first appeared as prose in *Offshoots IV, Writing from Geneva.*

For Karen Laudenslager McDermott, visual artist, the female form has been a persistent preoccupation. Now in her fifties, she is seeking expression for the strength, the power, and mystery in the body. American-born, Karen is also a photographer and a teacher of theater for adolescents. Her poems, essays, and stories are published in Switzerland and the United States. A member of The Geneva Writers' Group and The Leman Poetry Group, she divides her life between Amsterdam and Geneva.

"Les Femmes Sages"
Sculptures by Karen Laudenslager McDermott
Geneva, Switzerland

A NOTE FROM THE ARTIST: Some years ago, I began working with the idea of women warriors, women guardians. The result was an installation of fourteen strong female sculptures I titled "Les Femmes Gardiennes." The forms were made with clay and textile or paper, then fired in a primitive smoke kiln. They varied between ten and eighteen inches high. In 1999, these figures became older women, wise women, wrapped in layers of life experience, women with stories to tell—"Les Femmes Sages." They are actually wrapped in clay-cloth, clay-paper, and/or clay-lotus leaves, and fired very simply in a paper kiln or in a smoke kiln. The heads are carved apples.

Photographs by Karen Laudenslager McDermott.

Eulogy for My Best Friend
by Katherine C. Smith
Conway, South Carolina

*Y*ou were older and wiser than I. I needed time to grow. You were patient with me and gave me that time. I would never catch up with you and your wisdom, but you would learn patience in dealing with me and I would see by your example and learn. I used to hope I could one day walk in your shoes, but you taught me I had to learn to walk in my own, to seek truths, to know what is good, and to know that the future is promising. Today as I stand here with you, beside you, I am searching for that gift, seeking that discovery, stumbling on my feet. Even in death you taught me.

I learned humility.

You are quiet, still, beautiful, peaceful. I am glad you are, but I feel dead inside. I know you would be disappointed in me. You taught me to be strong, to accept the unacceptable, and to remember times when I persevered and there was success. As a human being, I hurt, and I struggle to remember the strength you taught me. I feel I will never see things in the same way again. Right now I know the sun will never feel as warm, the roses smell as sweet, or the day be as merry. The winter's chill will cut with a sharper edge. The laughter is hushed, the coughing quieted, the gasping breath stilled, and the light of your eyes dimmed. The sharing will be with myself and our memories.

I learned remembrance.

The stories are vivid memories. They have to be a part of you because that's the way you lived your life, spent your legacy, and shared experiences. You discovered life, understanding that it was a mystery. Believing this, you still lived spontaneously from the present time that always seemed an unpredictable place. You learned to accept the impossible and bear the intolerable.

I learned to cope.

You learned, broadened your horizons, and you were always indignant about injustices in the world and in your family. Some of your days were spent experimenting with life, wondering how, why, or if you fit in. For you, life was like playing cards: you could always play a poor hand well. You trusted life to be good to you, and it had an uncanny way of responding—maybe not always as you chose, but with a response anyway.

I learned to be resilient.

You taught me how to understand myself, listen to my inner self, keep in touch with my heart, to listen to the silence and appreciate it. You taught me sharing because your soul and heart served as a pantry. It was always stocked to feed the mind, nourish the soul, and fill the spirit with laughter. You taught me to soak up life, smile at the world, and feel the power of my own acceptance. You always had a way of putting a positive spin on things. You taught me to appreciate myself and the gifts my own life brought to others. You taught me to find happiness in nature and its gifts, see the serenity in the ever-changing sea, and feel the icy breath on the mountain tops.

I learned to listen to nature.

When cancer pronounced its claim on your body, you and I spoke often of Kubler-Ross's statement, "Learn to get in touch with silence within yourself. Know that everything in this life has a purpose." You taught me to be grateful for the good and the bad choices I'd made. You taught me to get in touch with myself and appreciate my own uniqueness, to know I was my own friend, and to know that I deserved peace.

I learned to know myself.

You learned to accept your illness and you worked from that point forward. When I was angry about your disease, you often reminded me that death was a natural predator, so I would have to accept death as well as life. Often times I would go by your house and you'd be gone to lunch, struggling to have some normalcy in your chaotic world. I was glad you were out, but sad because I knew one day the absence would be permanent. I tried to figure out what to do without you, and I couldn't. I tried to ignore the illness, and I could. I tried to put away the obvious, and I could. I was human and that was a lesson also.

I learned to pretend.

Who would validate me? Who would listen to my stories of triumph and defeat that I always made funnier because you enjoyed them so much? You always said you lived through me. Near the end, I often wondered if you realized I embellished sometimes to make you laugh. You often called me the angel from hell because I would make you get up and be a part of life when life seemed to have escaped you on your bad days. I am not sure who this masquerade was for—me or you? I wasn't even able to tell you how much I loved you. I couldn't climb outside myself to let you know. We were friends, like sisters. Surely you knew. I have to know you knew. We always had an understanding that transcended normal relationships. We didn't have to baby-sit our friendship. That's why it was so special.

I learned to accept.

Your zest for life was my spark. You taught me to be the change, not wait for it. You taught me that the power lies within each of us. I learned that, as life presents problems, I had a choice to use them as stumbling blocks or stepping stones.

I learned independence.

There was magic about us. There was always something about who we had been, who we were, and who we had become. There was a quiet trust, a bond, a belief in fairy tales and magic, but always with a sense of who we needed to be. You gave me the lessons of caring, cherishing, thinking, loving, and connecting. I will always miss you, cherish you, think of you, love you, and connect with you. I have faith. I know you are there.

I learned you will always be just a heartbeat away.

Katherine C. Smith is a high school teacher with twenty-five years experience. She is a feisty parent of two children and one grandson, living large, single, independent, strong, eccentric—and proud of it. She lives by the phrase "carpe diem" and does seize the day. She is an only child with a best friend who died, thus this poem. She is at work on her first book of poetry, a curriculum guide, and a children's picture book.

Section 3

Women's Circles

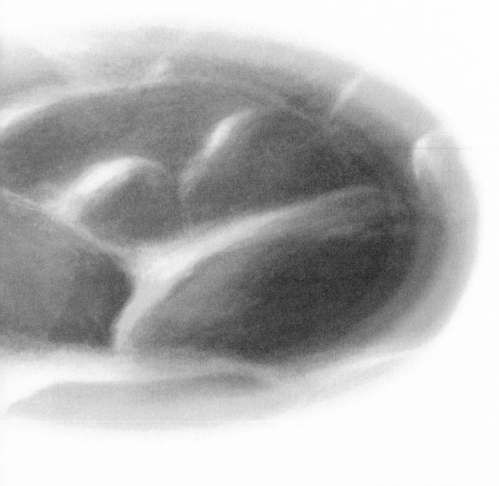

Beauty Marks
by Joyce Brady
San Francisco, California

*G*oing to the Beauty Parlor was never a luxury for me. It was a necessity; it shaped my life, not just my hair. It was in that place of beauty where I was taught a woman's way of living. It was in that place, where women were cared for, that I was able to recall memories and retrieve parts of myself. The Beauty Parlor was where I received counsel, praise, and attention. It was also where I expressed grief, anger, and joy. It was a place where black women gathered together, literally by appointment and symbolically by spiritual need. It was a place of wisdom and beauty marks.

My need for a hair dresser began after Mom's hospitalization, when my sister and I went to live with our father. At seven years old, I was suddenly wearing crooked braids with uneven parts. I was also feeling scared and nervous in my new home. My paternal relatives were silent about my mom because she was in a mental institution. Her name was never mentioned except in hushed voices. I felt alone even in the school yard filled with children.

For special occasions, or when money was available, I was sent around the corner to a Beauty Parlor on Amsterdam Avenue. There I got my hair washed, combed, and braided. Once, while my hair was being washed, my eyes filled with tears. It was not because of the water temperature, but because I began to feel scared again. I shut my eyes and tried to hold back the tears. When the water was turned off, I heard the hairdresser's quiet voice say to another woman as she looked at me, "This is a sensitive one." She then patted my hair dry and wiped the tears off my face.

Such a simple true statement instead of the usual teasing phrase I heard from my relatives, "You are such a cry baby." I continued crying.

She gave me a wet towel to wash my face and asked me, "Aren't you Bill Brady's daughter? "

I nodded, yes.

She said that I was lucky to have such a good father to take care of me. She said Dad had told her that I looked just like my mother, that I had her thick, long hair. "Your mother must be a beautiful woman."

I lifted my head and looked straight into the mirror and found the hairdresser's eyes. My fear lessened and I felt the sadness.

I missed my mother. Every Saturday night Mom had always washed and comb-twisted my hair into Shirley-Temple curls. Afterward I would jump, dance, and sing like Shirley Temple. At the end of my performance, Mom would clap her hands, pick me up, and give me a kiss.

Now another woman was washing my hair, and that released a dam of tears in me—safe away from my relatives' knowledge. I didn't know why, but I felt a lot better. This was a place of comfort for me, a place that dispensed little doses of truth and appreciation. This was a place where my tears were seen and understood, a place where I received a beauty mark of acceptance.

In 1978 I relocated from New York City to San Francisco with my two teenage children. After the usual school placement activities, finding a place to live, and checking out various job recommendations, I walked downtown in search of that special woman's place. I needed a place to connect, a Beauty Parlor. It was crucial because I did not have close friends or any extended family in the Bay Area. I saw a sign on Post Street that said "Soul Scissors" and went upstairs to make an appointment. From my first visit, while sitting in the midst of women, I intuitively knew that I was in the right place. The energy in the parlor centered around a young, wise hairdresser named Doris. She was the magnet that attracted women of all ages, a gatekeeper for women stories, the central support line for this community of women. She gave me the history of black women's experiences in San Francisco that anchored me in my transition from New York City.

In 1982 I felt a strong need to portray artistically the intimacy among women in the Beauty Parlor, especially the atmosphere of "chair healing" and group ritual. I saw how special the women felt as they reached the final chair in their ritual. It was here that a lot of individual attention was given, and many times it was an intimate moment. The chair also represented the fact that you were about to leave the parlor.

For six weeks, I talked to and photographed women in Doris's Beauty Parlor. In the darkroom I loved seeing the faces emerge in the developing tray and feeling the essence of their stories. At the end of the project, during a Sunday tea, the photographs were exhibited at the Beauty Parlor.

For the next twenty-one years, I have traveled like a nomad over city streets and bridges, following Doris whenever she moved her location. For the past seven years, the women's community has settled in the garden shop of Doris's private home. Whenever I enter the garden path leading to the French doors of the parlor, I feel energized. The energy comes from more than a general connection with the women; it comes from being in this place of freedom and knowing. I never know what the morning theme will be or which of the women will play a major part in the discussion. I only know that Doris is the initiator, facilitator, keeper, and synthesizer of the women's stories.

This Beauty Parlor has been my black women's internet. All areas of expertise and life's experiences are available to me as I click on to the appointment page. Many major decisions in my life were first reviewed at the Beauty Parlor—not necessarily overtly, but through the insight I gained as I listened to the women. The women's stories shifted, reshaped, and sustained me. All the important markers in my life were acknowledged in the Beauty Parlor: marriage, motherhood, diplomas, college degrees, and travel. It was also the place where I received emotional support and advice when I got divorced, raised teenagers, cared for an injured son, and coped with family addictions.

I have emerged from a sense of separation as a motherless child and have become a part of a strong multigenerational community of black women that I have easy access to on a bimonthly basis. They are voices of the mothers, sisters, daughters, and granddaughters in my life.

Whenever I want to celebrate a special occasion, all the good wishes begin at the Beauty Parlor. A room full of women is there to send me smiles, hand waves, and congratulations. The Beauty Parlor is a place to receive truth serum, professional advice, technical information, relaxation, and deep sleep. It is an open forum that encourages truth-telling, laughter, and unique voices. It is a place where lies are uncovered because there is not a lie worth living. It is a place for young girls to hear the experience of older women, a place for teen-agers to express their aspirations and struggles. It is a safe place where secrets are told because there is no secret too terrible to tell.

The Beauty Parlor was the place where I began as a small child to hear and feel the truth of my life, the place where I gathered from women what I needed and made it into my own mark of beauty.

Dedicated to all the wise women who left their beauty marks and to the keepers of their stories, Miss Mannings and Doris Baptiste.

Joyce Brady is a health educator, poet, and photographer. She facilitates "circles of wise women" using poetry and symbolism as vehicles to cultivate a remembrance of Self. She is working on her first book.

A Place for Me
by Apple Guinn
Key West, Florida

W omen

Changing

Me

Teaching, to dare, to seek, to grow

   Women

   Guiding

   Me

Nodding, to affirm, to welcome, to truth

   Women

   Knowing

   Me

Listening, to soothe, to stillness, to hear

   Women

   Inviting

   Me

Calling, to courage, to nature, to become

   Women

   Protecting

   Me

Supporting, to cry, to fear, to heal

   Women

   Cherishing

   Me

Nurturing, to self, to center, to voice

Women

Embracing

Me

Smiling, to moon, to darkness, to joy

Women

Loving

Me

Sharing, to give, to dance, to breathe

Women

Showing

Me

Lighting, to balance, to path, to home

Women

Connecting

Me

Surrounding, to roots, to circle, to infinity

Women

Acknowledging

Me

Sustaining, to women, to us, to me

For me, For us, For women

Apple Guinn, twenty-seven, is a writer, poet, activist, and currently works as a sales associate. She was born and raised in New York. She now lives in Key West where she is beginning her first novel and awaiting the birth of her first child.

Seeing in to me.
by Maranú Gascoigne
Stoneyford, Lisburn, Northern Ireland

A NOTE FROM THE AUTHOR: Each year in spring and autumn, I offer a retreat for women to come away from the treadmills of their daily lives and routines and enter the cave . . . literally. The retreat house is accessible only through a cave. I call these retreats "Women Keeping Silence Together." Although I am a counsellor, I do these primarily for myself. I believe that we cannot heal separately, so I welcome my women travellers to join me to drink from our own wells. Each retreat has opened me up more and more. I have risked setting down the masks that keep me from deep intimacy and have discovered new depths within my own womanhood. These poems have emerged out of this journey to become a full-bodied woman.

In the company of love
I break the bread of my life.
And you receive me.

I open my heart.
A tear drops
like a silent snow flake,
and you hold me.

Together we concede to love.
Unhesitatingly a symphony plays
between the shores of our souls.

Beauty and generosity
meet here and touch.
There is no hiding place.

And so it is, the heart beats,
the breath breathes.
And God is known.

Women knowing women.

*T*hey came, three generations of women,
the Maiden, the Mother, the Crone.
Travellers from distant lands,
led by a holy longing to be held.

We sat circled by rough-hewn stones.
The mouth of the ocean lapped our shores
as we waited for women's wisdom.
Silently she spilled over, and we drank deep from our own well.
Fountains of pure water flowing, cleansing and renewing.

We held each other in this holding place,
we brought our wounded innocence to be touched.
Here we howled the burdens of our wombs.

Woman being birthed, woman being held, woman holding woman.
This is my body.

Woman spilling out her grief, woman wiping her tears.
This is my blood.

Woman singing, woman dancing belly to belly.
This is my resurrection.

Maranú Gascoigne is a four-year-old discovering how to be grown up. Her Celtic name means "woman who watches at the well." Together with her husband, Eolath, she is building a "Peace Labyrinth" in their garden. If ever you are in Northern Ireland, please come and walk it. (By the way, I am forty-one!)

"Sunrise"
Painting by Jean Boelan Gascoigne
Stoneyford, Lisburn, Northern Ireland

A NOTE FROM THE ARTIST: "Sunrise" was captured in the wakening moment on the shores of Roisbeg Donegal. Capturing the breaking of dawn and the rising of the sun . . . There my soul embraced the beauty and light as she unfolded before my eyes.

Jean Boelan Gascoigne is a professional artist and therapist residing in Ireland with her partner, Jo. "Sunrise" is one of the many "Soul Paintings" Jean has created. She also enjoys creating "Soul Paintings" for solo and group exhibition, the corporate market, and private commissions. She has trained in using art in a therapeutic setting, facilitating individuals and groups on their own soul journeys.

Retreat
by Morna Finnegan
Armagh, Ireland

*U*p at the top of the forest,
hidden among a thousand trees,
leaning out over the precipice,
lives an old oak.

Most days I don't go
along the narrow, needled path,
to stand with the wind
and the mist,
to breathe his air.
But always I know
he lives there
in the frilled shelter
of his own shade.
And the knowing
of something as real
can be a sustenance
to the mind's eye.
For all my imagination,
the tree is a strength
my fingers trust,
a physical manifestation
of love
with his course
and creaturely skin.

So for years, I carried
a vision
of the women
there might be.
Somehow, somewhere to
weep and to wake,
to grieve
and to celebrate with me.
Always a fabrication,
always a yearning,
always a dream.
The one opening
into myself
I could not find.
We grew up unmothered,
all of us,
in these days of the masculine.
Detached from the web
of old knowledge
spun out of the womb-time,
women's time.
Forbidden to learn
the old wisdom words
and the gestures
that blessed her
so long.

As they burned
and they beat
and they cheated the daughters
out of the grandmother's
songs,
a culture, a language,
an archetype
was washed from the shores
of our minds.
But doesn't it always
lie dormant within you,
keening
beneath your own eyes?
And I've travelled my life
in search of an image
mapped on to the cells
of my soul
of a circle of women
breathing together—
the Maiden,
the Mother,
the Crone.
Telling myself it was foolish,
telling myself it could never
be real.

But among the red caves
of cushendun,
while the wild sea
howled outside,
and the wild sea rose
at last
within me,
wasn't I held like a child?
Wasn't I raised
by the arms of thirteen
sisters, out of the cold,
and rocked like a feather
contained by the wind,
and crooned and patted to rest?
And when the time came,
didn't I offer the same
soft hands of solace?
And everything is now
changed
forever.
Everything will be new.
Within my own body
I carry a place
to return to,
for the dark days.
What has been touched
by the fingers
lives on as a truth
within us always.

I stumble up through
the forest,
I come to the grove
where those women wait.
This is the revolution,
of return.
Fierce in the silence
of gathering here,
where only the candles burn,
women will remember
who we are.

Creating ourselves as real
again,
in the temple
of the soft power;
each one of us sheds
her amnesiac skin.
Each one of us
bows,
and steps in.

Written after a women's retreat based on Circle Of Stones.
Dedicated to Phyllida, Seabheanna, and Clare.

Morna Finnegan is twenty-nine years old and originally from Armagh, Ireland. She currently lives with her partner in Belfast, and her writing is a central part of her life. The women's retreats she has attended have profoundly shaped her personal journey and are part of a life-long interest in women's culture and empowerment.

Circle of Women
by Linda Wilkinson
Joelton, Tennessee

How might my life have been different . . . if there had been a place . . . a place of women . . . where I could go . . . and sit with these women . . . some older, some younger . . . and be heard . . . both the day-to-day ordinary, the joys, the sorrows, and the deep longings of my soul? How might my life have been different . . . if these women . . . some older, some younger . . . had sat beside me, listening intently and nodding intently at my sharing? And how would my life have been different . . . if these women then shared their experience, their strength, and their hope. How would my life have been different?

I know exactly how, for this is my experience:

I was in the middle of my thirtieth year when I first joined the circle of women, drawn together by common life experiences. When I heard their stories, I wept, for they spoke my heart: my fears, my pain, my sorrow, my hopes and dreams—which at that point in my life seemed out of reach. As I sat and wept, they reached out to me, embraced me, held me, encouraged my tears, and encouraged me to keep coming back.

And so I did. Week after week, I joined this circle of women. Week after week, I wept. And slowly, after hearing them speak my life through their stories, I began to trust: trust these women, trust my self, trust my experiences, trust my inner voice, trust that one day I, too, would be able to have what they had. Soon, I could speak the words of my story through my tears. And my tears became intermingled with laughter as I recovered the feeling of Joy.

I learned about anger: it is my friend, my protector. I learned to trust my inner self, rather than denying even its strongest callings.

I learned to listen carefully to its slightest whisperings, for in that is the truest connection to my Self.

I learned to trust the God that I now understood.

I came to believe there is hope for my life. As the days, weeks, and
months passed, I noticed myself coming to life.

I came to know the woman that I am today:
caring, gentle, passionate, whole.

I have a whole range of emotions that no longer control my life.

I have a deepened spirituality and a deeper connection
with my Inner Self.

I have a voice.

I listen.

I learn.

I was reborn into this circle of women who rejoice in my growth
and continue to walk with me.

*Linda Wilkinson was born and raised outside Boston, Massachusetts, and currently
lives outside of Nashville, Tennessee, with her husband and soul-mate, Steven. Early
dubbed a "country mouse," she has always been a lover of nature. Nurse practitioner by
profession, she is currently studying massage therapy. She retreats often to the woods
and to her "circle of women," finding balance, grace, joy, and centeredness. She and her
husband wait with anticipation for the birth of their twins.*

The Circle of Life
by *Zanada Moody*
Bronx, New York

$\mathcal{W}$hen I think of my life,
I think of a circle.

It seems as if my life has been an evolution.
A start as small as a speck of lint.
Crawling. Toddling. Stepping.
In tiny windows in my mind,
I view hundreds of well-kept memories.
Memories old.
Memories new.
Will I ever know where or how it all came to be?
My struggle to answer is part of my everlasting evolution.

In the beginning,
I had to make a decision.
A decision to live or to die.
Bad habits and choices had left me weak.
Time had raced by me so rapidly!
I had a beginning,
but there seemed to be no end.
I had to make a decision.
A decision to live.
Broken dreams rebuilt.
Heart and mind mended.
Knees bloody and brushed off.

I came to believe:
I am more than a mother.
I am more than a wife,
or even a daughter.
I am a woman of color
with immeasurable knowledge
of which even I didn't know!
I am a woman whom I can love today.

Sisters,
Round and smooth in places.
        Like our bodies.
Hard and jagged.
        Like times in our lives.
Deep and piercing.
        Like our cries during childbirth.
Strong and never ending.
        Like our Love and our Spirit.
Sisters,
We are all the same and yet so vastly different.
        We are the circle of life.

Zanada Moody, born in Queens, now resides in the Bronx. She has five children, two grandchildren, and a challenging life's journey that keeps her growing and writing. Life is not over, as she once felt . . . but is she ready for the good things life and God have to offer? Her writing helps her explore these questions and answers.

Section 4

Women's Wisdom . . .
Women's Vision

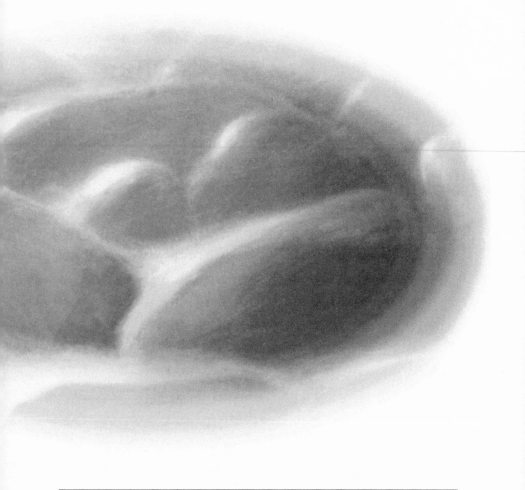

What If
by Maril Crabtree
Kansas City, Missouri; Naples, Florida

$\mathcal{W}$hat if
god is
a room filled with women
finding ways to get done
what needs to be
done in this world
with their

> webweaving
> taletelling
> joysharing
> painhealing
> ways?

these things we'd see:
unity of
purpose
diversity of

> path
> peace
> laughter
> huge hugs
> child's play

we'd gentle
our way
into the future

Maril Crabtree is a writer, energy healer, and environmental educator who draws constant inspiration from wonderful women friends in her "hometowns" of Kansas City and Naples, as well as other cities around the globe. Her poems, essays, and articles have been published in a number of journals, magazines, and anthologies.

Asking. For My Life.
by *Mary Roberts*
Carlisle, Massachusetts

"What do women want?"

In the Arthurian legend "Sir Gawain and the Loathsome Lady," King Arthur must find the correct answer to this question within a week or lose his life. He asks every woman he encounters and gets what he thinks are some terrific answers: honor and respect; protection and being provided for; a sense of home and family; being loved and desired. But on the seventh day, Arthur is told the correct answer: women want sovereignty—the right to chose, to have one's own way.

I am captivated with this answer. After all, if no one honors or respects me, I can respect myself. If no one loves me, I can love myself. If no one provides for me, I can support myself. The power to make my own choices is mine alone.

One August day, I shared the story enthusiastically with a friend. But he said, "I don't agree with that answer." Surprised, I asked why. He lowered his voice. "What women most want is security . . . and a man to provide that security and to make decisions for them." He went on more forcefully. "If you ask ten women, any ten women, nine out of ten would give the answer I just told you."

For a moment, I was too shocked to reply. At last I said, "What women do you know? I don't know very many women who would give that answer." Then I heard myself making a promise, before I could even consider its implications. "I am going to ask—not ten women, but a hundred women. And I bet I won't find nine women in one hundred who want what you say they want."

I was determined to prove my point. Also, I was intrigued with the process of asking individual women want they want. So I began the task of asking one hundred women, "What do you want for yourself ?"

I started with the mothers of my daughter's friends. A few days later, we left on a family vacation to Australia. Emboldened by the enthusiastic responses back home, I approached a stranger standing in the Los Angeles airport. To my surprise, she took the time to give me a thoughtful reply. My quest had begun.

I found I didn't always have the energy to ask the question. But whenever I felt receptive enough and bold enough, I asked strangers, sales people, friends, and relatives. I asked women in private homes, at a wedding, in a hospital, at the gym, and in the grocery store. Over the next two-and-a-half years, I connected with one hundred women who varied in age, education, profession, race, and economic level. Each encounter lasted from one minute to an hour, and the average time was fifteen minutes. Occasionally I would share pieces from my own life. Only one woman refused to answer. Only two women—one in extreme poverty, the other with a physical disability—most wanted financial security provided by a man.

In the Sydney airport, I asked a distinguished elderly woman about to board a plane. Clad in a tweed suit and with silver hair framing her dignified face, she replied simply, "World peace." As she walked through the departure gate I stood in silence. For a moment, I put myself in the mind set of a world with no fighting or hatred. I imagined people getting along with one another and being able to trust one another. I felt safe. Suddenly, I grew hopeful about living in such a world.

Later that day, my husband and adolescent son pulled me aside and said I was embarrassing them. My husband said, "You are making these women uncomfortable. They don't want to talk to you."

I said, "But they keep talking to me, and they don't tell me to go away."

At our next airport, Cairns, I approached two South African girls on a sports tour. As they answered, their teammates became curious, and they, too, began discussing the question. They wanted different things for themselves and didn't always agree with each other's opinions. After a time, I caught a glimpse of my son, sitting quietly on the periphery, listening.

Across the way, I saw a woman sweeping the floor. I noticed her worn-out clothes and her limp, stringy hair. After hearing my question, she gazed downward, leaned with her hands folded on her broom and said, "I most want to make life easier, to have enough and save some, to not fall behind, and to not have to struggle." Looking at her I could feel a heavy weight on my shoulders. I felt suffocated . . . as if there were no way out and this women had no options.

Over in the sitting area were two divorced professional women traveling together. Dressed for hiking, they exuded a zest for life. To my question one replied, "I want to retain a sense of wonder, and to feel content with and to be at peace with myself." I thanked them, boarded a small plane with my family and flew to a remote island on the Great Barrier Reef. Within minutes I was knee-deep in clear, sparkling, blue-green water. The coral and the vibrant fish glistened in the sun's rays. I became a part of this underwater magnificence. This was the wonder and contentment she meant!

Riding a tourist train through the sugar-cane fields of Queensland, I met a young dentist with her husband and two happy, energetic toddlers. She most wanted: "a reliable full-time nanny. It is exhausting and disruptive to drive my children to day care. I need help at home."

Every few moments, she turned to check on her children. Watching her, I remembered a typical morning with my own toddlers, back in Virginia. I showered, dressed, ate breakfast, loaded my school bag and the baby's bag in the car, woke the children, dressed them while I sang and talked to them with one eye on the clock, fed them, put on their jackets, hats, and mittens, went to the car, then suddenly darted back upstairs for a diaper change. I, too, longed for a caregiver to arrive at my house and take over my maternal duties when I worked, but I couldn't afford child care in my home. Unable to rest when I was tired, forced to fit so much activity into a few daily hours, I felt I was hanging by a slender thread.

Watching this capable but harried woman in Queensland, I realized one reason I had learned to ignore myself. Given the magnitude of my job as mother, and the paucity of support, I felt I could not afford to acknowledge my inner needs.

A Greek pharmacist in her mid-twenties helped me in a Sydney apothecary. She looked me in the eye and spoke with certainty and authority, "I want to find power in my career and to find a balance of power in a love relationship."

"Wow!" I thought, "This is the kind of answer I'm looking for!" Later I mused, "This woman is twenty-six. When I was twenty-six, I was in a fog. I was planning to get married and I was achievement-oriented. I made decisions I might not have made had I been clearer about my priorities."

By now I had reached my half-way mark, and I had not answered the question for myself. What did I most want? What a hard question! How on earth did fifty women answer so quickly and easily? One quiet morning when my children were at school, I wrote, "Complete self-love and acceptance; the feeling that no matter what I do, I am good enough."

Later, my family took a day trip to Nantucket. On the ferry, a professional woman replied, "I want a good man who will respect me. I have material things." Here was someone who provided for herself. All she wanted from a man was respect. Looking out over the calm water, I nodded in understanding.

One night I entered a restaurant kitchen where several women were hard at work. A waitress said, "I am a battered-woman survivor, raise three children, work three jobs, and go to school part-time. I want to be in my profession of choice in five years. I also want to be a force in my children's lives so they make a difference in the world." I asked her where she found her security. She put her hand on her solar plexus and said, "You're looking at my security. I'm it!"

By the time I had connected with eighty-two women, I found myself in the hospital for minor foot surgery. I lay on an examination table surrounded by a nurse, a pre-med student, and a medical assistant. We waited for the dermatologist to arrive and perform the operation. Finally she rushed in, apologizing, "I had to take a moment to pump my breasts between appointments." But the doctor took the time to hear the nine-teen-year-old Haitian medical assistant answer my question. "Right now I want to get through undergrad and graduate school," she said. "I know what I want to do, and I don't want it to overwhelm me. I love medicine, but everything I have to do to get there is a long haul. I want to get through it. But I love my job as medical assistant. It is my compensation when I am discouraged with school. When I get to this job, it reminds me that this is where I want to be."

Hearing her, I flashed back to being an undergraduate. My European history professor told me, "You could become a good historian if you develop a writing style." For years, I had wondered, "Why didn't I follow through in studying history?" But now I realized the truth. To have developed my own style, I would have needed to have known who I was and what I was about. I had been so highly rewarded for my achievement in other fields that I hadn't paused to find my own voice.

One day my husband, daughter, and I picked my son up at a friend's house. From there, we had planned to go out to eat. I went inside the house to get directions to the restaurant. I came out of the house and discovered two extra boys and their bikes in the car. I asked my husband, "What's going on?" I then learned that, without consulting me, my husband had changed our dinner plans to give the boys a ride to their home.

Two years before, I would have been furious . . . and said nothing. Later in the evening I would have called a friend to vent, then eaten some cookies. But, instead, the memory of the Greek pharmacist ("I want a balance of power in a relationship"), the battered woman survivor ("You're looking at my security. I'm it!"), and the professional woman from the ferry ("I want a good man who will respect me") passed through my mind. To my surprise, I heard myself calmly saying, "Boys, our family is going out to dinner. Could one of your parents drive you?" The boys found another ride home.

Later my husband and I argued about this moment. He said I was being selfish. I said, "When family decisions are made, I want my voice to be considered also." From that day on I took a new place within my family. I insisted on being treated more respectfully.

Recently, I discovered that I had asked ninety-seven women what they most want. Carefully, I chose my last three women, but one proved unavailable.

One night, still lacking a final woman to ask, I attended the concert of two former music students and their backup band. Katryna, my student from third to sixth grade, was the lead singer. Now tall and thin with long dark hair, she was a commanding presence as she danced with her long arms above her head. Afterward she and I sat on the stage steps, recalling how I had given her recorder lessons and taught her to read music. Feeling the warmth between us, I spontaneously asked, "What do you most want for yourself?"

She thought a moment before answering. "Nerissa and I are sisters," she said. "All our lives we wanted to be singers. Every day now I wake up and am grateful that we are doing exactly what we wanted to do."

"Amazing!" I thought. "Katryna is the one-hundredth woman and she wants . . . what she has."

As I began to write about my "survey," I wanted to answer the question one more time. I realized that my earlier answer had been colored by my desire to give the best possible answer. I wanted to be sure I was "right" by surveying the other women, then comparing my answer to theirs.

But now I just wanted my own answer, one that comes from within me. How it was graded simply didn't matter any more.

What do I want for myself? I want to be at home with myself in silence and in stillness, to honor my basic goodness, to believe I am worthy and whole, and to carry this inner peace with me when I am in the world.

Throughout my life, I realized, I hid in the hyperactivity of accomplishment. I behaved like a school child who pushes to be first in line. I toiled, strove, and rarely rested. I overlooked the reality that all the children, no matter where their place in line, arrive at their next class within moments of each other. I had expended so much energy to be in the forefront, when being just nearby might have been more enjoyable and less costly to my authentic self.

How do I know this particular quest is over? On warm weather days, I sit on my garden bench and eat my lunch. This is the bench I bought eight years ago . . . but never sat on until now. I notice the trees, flowers, and wild-life in my yard.

One day this summer, I became still enough to really notice my dog, Tasha, lying in the sun in her usual spot by the yew. She lay there serenely, and I wondered how that felt. I lay on the grass to find out. I savored the sun's warmth and the gentle breeze. I felt one with the sun and the breeze and my breath.

I was unaware of a car driving up the road, until I heard my neighbor's voice, "Are you okay?"

I lifted my head slowly and called back, "I'm fine!"

Looking back on that afternoon, I realize I have never been better.

Mary Roberts is a musician, writer, athlete, and environmental healer. For twenty-one years in the Washington, D.C. area, she taught and performed music, got married, gave birth to a boy, and adopted a girl from Korea. In 1995 Mary moved to Carlisle, Massachusetts, and established a private piano studio and founded the Western Ladies Singles Tennis League. She recently graduated from the Western School of Feng Shui and is studying how the application of Feng Shui pinciples in schools affects children's learning. Mary enjoys yoga, meditation, Chi Gong, and nature walks. At age fifty, she learned a yoga head stand!

The Copper Child and Her Auntie Goddesses
by Donna Lee Hill
Laguna Niguel, California

Once, a long time ago, a Baby Goddess was born. Her family, including several Auntie Goddesses, was overjoyed at her birth, and the two Grandmother Goddesses hovered over her crib, most often searching through her soft caplet of head fuzz for colors of copper or earth. You see, it was very important to know the color of the Baby Goddess's hair because that would tell the world which of the Grandmother Goddess's lineage would flow forth into the world.

One glorious day a Grandmother Goddess and the Mother Goddess saw a tiny glimmer of copper in the finely spun strands of hair now dusting over the Baby Goddess's tiny petal ears. Great hoots and cheers were heard in the earth, in the stone, the waters, and the sky as the copper-haired Grandmother Goddess learned that *her* lineage would flow forth—the Baby Goddess would walk the earth with her Grandmother's copper locks glowing for all to see! (There was not just a little pleasure in that for her).

As the Baby Goddess grew, her hair brightened and glowed as fire does from the sun. Other women commented to the child and her mother about its exquisite color. "Do you dye your child's hair?" one asked, sure that none could have such special color naturally.

Wide-eyed with wonder at such a question, the Child Goddess heard her Mother chuckle, "Oh no, her color is natural."

Of course and over time, the copper-haired Child Goddess learned her coloring was a treasure, and she so connected that to her very identity. From the deepest core of her being, she was of the glimmering streams of copper that run through the stones in the earth, that reflect in Autumn rivers, when the brilliant orange, gold, and red leaves dress the forests, that flame the sky with brilliant fire at sun's setting. The Copper Goddess Child was of the earth. She was happiest and most at peace when she played in the woods among the trees and wildflowers, rocks and earth, water and sky.

Sadness began seeping into her heart when people around her were un-happy or angry. She did not understand what was so wrong with her that it could so displease the elders or cause another child to be mean to her. She did not understand why some criticized or fought with each other. This was not how a Goddess Child thought it would be! Oh, it wasn't always that way, but it was *enough* that way to frighten her. The more she grew, the less she glowed. She knew she was to walk the earth casting warmth and glowing all about, but much to her dismay, her coppery brilliance became tarnished from sadness and fear here and there.

Oh, her beautiful golden core still burned deeply and kept her life spirit alive; she just had to be very careful who got to *see* it. Oh yes, she had learned that some would try to tarnish it more if her coppery glow shone a little too brightly.

At least some Auntie Goddesses still made her feel most special and adored, so the Child Goddess's glow would particularly fire up when around them, and warmth would spread outward from each of them to each other. These Auntie Goddesses and the Child Goddess were so connected, the warmth from their inherited and brilliant copper-colored life spirit melded their hearts together. Something was still quite right about her, and she adored warming herself in their love. It fed her own copper fire inside in a very special way indeed.

Then one year, the Elder Auntie Goddess got very angry and stopped speaking to another Auntie Goddess! The Grandmother Goddess even fought with them—except she didn't fight with the one Auntie Goddess to whom the elder one wasn't speaking. What could one possibly *do* to make Women Goddesses not speak to each other? And for tens of years! How could Women Goddesses, including the copper-haired Grandmother God-dess who was the head of their very lineage, get *that* angry with each other?

Oh my, something was very, very wrong in the Goddess world. The Child Goddess still loved all her family, but she couldn't be with all of them together anymore because the Elder Auntie Goddess wouldn't speak to another, and the Grandmother Goddess wouldn't speak to the Elder Goddess! The coppery child received only bits and pieces of the once-whole family. At least she could still see each of them, she comforted herself.

But from then on, something was never allowed to be talked about amongst the Auntie Goddesses. And it had to do with *something* two of the Aunties had said to each other. And it was about the Grandmother Goddess.

The Child Goddess grew to be an adult, and this unspeakable divide in her family continued to gnaw at her heart. It was none of "her" business what the unspeakable was; that was just for the Grandmother and Auntie Goddesses to know—even though the Copper Child had to live with it and feel the separation among some of her favorite women people. But then one day the Grandmother Goddess died, leaving the Auntie Goddesses and the now-grown Child Goddess with the still-unresolved unspeakable.

The Copper Goddess couldn't abide the silence any longer, so she started to speak of it. She investigated and asked questions. Her golden soul knew that light must shine on its truth. Her relationship with her beloved Auntie Goddess deserved it and needed it. She had to know the truth, whatever it was. "Enough with this!" the Copper Child Goddess insisted, as her patience and forced silence wore mighty thin indeed . . . and her copper glow seemed to brighten just a little bit more at such a pronouncement.

Well, talk about fire! The sparks came from very deep in some of the Auntie Goddesses, once the Child Goddess asked and asked and talked and talked! "This is *not* to be pulled up after this long!" one shrieked. "Some things are better left unsaid!" cried another. "It's long since been buried. *Why* are you digging it up?" they wailed.

"Because it is *not* buried," the Copper Goddess said strongly. "Because my Auntie Goddess's character is being questioned year after year after year. Because the truth should be known. Because my relationship with my special Auntie Goddess needs to know. That's why I'm talking about it."

And you know what? The Auntie Goddesses didn't even know what had really happened! Oh yes, they got snippets of information and an accusation thrown out by the Elder Auntie Goddess, but not one of them ever knew what the whole and true story was.

Except the copper-haired Child Goddess would not give up. In some intuitive way, she knew her Auntie Goddess, who had always been there for her, who had always been open and compassionate—even to the one who wounded her with the falsehood—who had the strength not to be bitter and hateful even though she had been wrongly accused and doubted, was loving and good. The Child Goddess unfolded the layers of the story, pouring out her glowing coppery light over the creases and crevices of her Auntie Goddess's life event for all the family to hear. The truth showed her to be the loving and compassionate Goddess that the Child Goddess always felt she was, not the unreliable and not-so-nice one she had been accused of being by the Elder Auntie Goddess.

For the second time, great hoots and cheers were felt in the earth, in the stone, the waters, and the sky as the younger Goddess, who had inherited the copper strands and glowed within, learned and spread the truth about her older and most special Auntie Goddess. The Copper Child Goddess and the Special Auntie Goddess were warmed and deeply connected by each other's gift of love. The final coppery strand was allowed . . . finally . . . finally . . . to warm, to finish flowing forth, to meld their relationship . . . as copper does in a stone to finish its wholeness.

Donna Lee Hill, born (body and soul) in New England, currently lives on the "other" coast, in California with her adored husband and spoiled dog. She returned to college as an "older woman" and earned her Ph.D. in psychology and social behavior. Most important to her is treasuring life and sharing home with family and friends, so in her own good time, she is writing a third book, American Decency 101. *She freely encourages calling women "Goddesses!"*

The Keeper of the Faceless Women
by Reda Rackley
Carmel Valley, California

*Y*a nev'r know how these stories come about, but I think my Granny Grace's grandmother's grandmother passed this story on. I can remember sittin' at my Granny's feet watchin' her face as she told this story. It goes a somethin' like this:

A long, long time ago, there lived an old woman named Serephina. They say her face had so many wrinkles one could barely see her eyes. But you knew she saw everything. Now Serephina had another name. They called her "The Keeper of the Faceless Women."

Now you might ask yourself who or what is "The Keeper of the Faceless Women."

This is what my Granny said: "This old woman carry upon her face the life events of every woman born. One wrinkle, the birth of a newborn; another wrinkle, the loss of a lover; and yet another wrinkle, the violation of a woman's sweet body; and another wrinkle, her wedding day. Every emotion and feelin' a woman expressed and could not express lived upon that old woman's face. She carried within her the memories of the deepest loves and the darkest moments in a woman's life.

"The Keeper of the Faceless Woman was so old," Granny said, "and had so many wrinkles, you might think you was lookin' at an ancient rock a billion years old. She lived in cave hidden high in the mountains and hadn't shown her face or come out of that cave for an eternity, it seems like. They say she's been a-waitin' for her daughters to return, she's been a-preparin' the dark place. And lord, lord, her daughters always return, they have always found their way back to Her. They come a-draggin' their bones and bringin' their weary flesh behind them. They stumble into the hidden entrance to the cave and fall into the black silence. They have finally found the dark place, the quiet place, the place to surrender, to surrender, to let go, to let go. The tears begin to flow, tears they been waitin' to cry for an eternity.

"The Keeper of the Faceless Women just rocks and chants, 'Yes my daughter, yes my daughter, you home now, you home now. You finally made you way back. You just let that grief flow, little sister, let those tears cleanse your heart. And when you done cryin', honey, and you've empty yourself of all that they told you to be, you gonna find out what they been tryin' to keep from you all these years. You gonna find out you are a woman, a woman with passion, a woman with joy, a woman with purpose, a woman with a body to celebrate and, baby, you gonna find out you ain't got to hide your light no more. Cause 'dis little light of mine, I gonna let it shine, 'dis little light of mine, I gonna let it shine.

'Oh baby girl, you are bright, you are brilliant. Girl, I da old one, I can carry ya tears now. I can carry one more wrinkle on to 'dis old face. You don't have to carry that burden no more.

'You knew you had to find your way back to me and mourn and cry and cry and mourn. But, chile, there comes a time when you got to get on up. Get on up now, daughter, you got to walk back down that road, and you got to walk proud and haughty like. You got to walk like you got sparkling jewels between your thighs. You got to redefine what passion is, woman. You got somethin' to say, you got somethin' to do.

'I can carry your pain and your laughter, too. Girl, you ain't got to worry woe no mo'. Gonna lay down my burdens down by the riverside, down by the riverside, gonna lay down my burdens down by the riverside, ain't gone worry woe no more. You ain't got to worry woe no more.

'You are brilliant, girl. Let your light shine.' "

Reda Rackley is a cultural mythologist, writer, storyteller, and dancer. She has a passion for creating sacred space for women to explore ancient feminine wisdom using myth, ritual, and the body. She is currently facilitating a nine-month initiation for women, taking them to the caves to encounter "The Keeper of the Faceless Women." She is also teaching with Malidoma Some, elder and shaman of the Dagura tribe of West Africa.

Fear Not
by *Cheryl Anne Mohr*
Northumberland, Pennsylvania

Fear not my Sister
when you hear your heart call
you out of the separate
and into the All

Fear not when the rhythm
continually rises
and the predictable fills
with sudden surprises

Fear not when you learn
that you must go alone
So the voice speaking truth
to your soul is your own
and the face gazing at you
with utmost affection
and promise, none other
than your own reflection

Fear not when you see
the extent of illusion,
injustice, oppression,
unwanted intrusion

Fear not this journey
which leads to the Light
though it's path may meander
through perilous night

Fear not for your sisters
will be waiting there
in the Circle, with wisdom
and stories to share
of when they were called
and their drumsongs began
When their souls opened up
and revealed the great plan

Fear not your difference
for it is the same
as all of the others
who carry the flame
And all of the others
who marvel and know
where the wellsprings of Love
and Creation must flow

Fear not my Sister
the song of the Moon
or the mystery of
Her passionate tune

Fear not the stars
or the heat of the Sun
Who melts all the separate
into The One

Fear not the Wind
as She blows through your life
stirring up anguish and anger
and strife

For in love She has come
to whisk it away
and uncover the beauty
which beneath it does lay

Fear not your Truth
though some may oppose
See the evidence mount
as your love for all grows
So follow your heart
give your True Self a chance
Fear not my Sister . . .
join in the Dance!

Cheryl Anne Mohr loves words. Reading them, hearing them, feeling them. Singing them, speaking them, and most especially, writing them. Whether in the journals she keeps for her three children, songs she writes for people she loves, poems from the depths of her soul, prayers of Spirit, or silly real life stories, words have filled every corner of her life since she wrote her first poem in 1972 at the age of six. Cheryl believes that words are powerful and should be used to bring life and light, hope and healing to those who experience them.

Befriending My Angel of Death
by Diana C. Douglas
Vancouver, British Columbia, Canada

A NOTE FROM THE AUTHOR: The following is an exploration of my imaginings of a vibrant and ongoing relationship with my Angel of Death.

*A*t an earlier time in my life:

"Angel of Death." Whenever I see or hear these words, immediately I feel fear, I see darkness. I think of the Grim Reaper, I choose not to think any further. I know that I am not afraid of being dead; it is the way I might die that scares me. I know that I have this fear, and I feel helpless in the face of it. I turn away from it—feeling that I am living life, I am young, and illness and death are a long way off. Somewhere in me, I know that this fear stops me from living passionately, fully present.

*A*nd then one day:

I listen to *The Radiant Coat* by Clarissa Pinkola-Estes (author of *Women Who Run With the Wolves*). *The Radiant Coat* is a collection of myths and stories about Death from other cultures. In these cultures, Death is understood to be our great companion, midwifing us into this world at our births and transporting us out of this world at our deaths. As I listen, new possibilities arise in me.

And then I remember Judith Duerk's "How might your life have been different . . ." questions in the *Circle of Stones*, and I ask myself: How would my life be different if I were conscious of my Angel of Death? Further, how would I live my life differently if I knew my Angel of Death? If I *really* knew Her as my companion and guide, midwife and healer? If I attended to Her daily, asked for guidance, loved Her as a friend?

I want to get to know Her. So, I begin to imagine that I have been able to talk with my Angel of Death throughout my life. These conversations may be a re-writing of my history, or perhaps they are a bringing to consciousness of what was actually going on beyond my awareness.

*A*t my birth, my soul awaiting to enter my body:

"Oo-ee," my Angel of Death says. "And this is how it goes. You is out of Time now, and you has done a mighty fine job settin' up your plan. So this is what we do: at the perfect moment, jus' as that fine baby head comes out between your momma's legs and then the shoulder, and the baby turns upward, you see that place on the chest between the pretty li'l nipples. Jus' when you see that, I'll give you a sweet tap or maybe a shove and in you'll go. Now, let me tell you a thing or two about being in Time, in a body. In a baby's body. It's small. And you is so big, Honeychil'. You jus' go in there and tell me how it is. If you feel lost or stuck or sick in your belly, you jus' call on me."

*A*t my first birthday party with friends, age three:

It is a warm spring day. We are having a picnic lunch in the backyard. There is a small, weather-worn wooden table and four chairs, all a bit wobbly. My job is to put all the goodies on the table: four paper plates, four spoons, four shiny cardboard hats, four yellow balloons, four paper cups for milk. I like counting. My best friend, Jannie, and my brother are the people guests. That makes two. Then there's me. That makes three. And number four. I just know that I need to have another place . . . for whom? And then I hear:

"Hi there, Honeychil'. This is Blessing talkin'. What a party you is havin'! And I sure is glad to be here. Every day is special. And today is your day. You remember those first few months fittin' yourself into your pretty body. Hard work! You sure got somethin' to celebrate today. You is learning how to make yourself big and small in the body as need be. An' your friend, Jannie. She loves you since the beginning of Time . . ."

*D*uring childhood trauma:

"Oh Honeychil'," Blessing says, "you sure is in trouble. Let me love you up a bit, hug and hold you until you remember who you are. And then it's time for you to go back. Yes'm, Honeychil', you is not finished yet. I'm a-tellin' you, Bodylife and I jus' now had a talk. Bodylife say to me, 'Blessing, oh, Blessing, what are we to do with this one? Her experience down here is more than difficult, what with all this hurt.' And I says to Bodylife, and I says to you: 'Life, you must let her grow and go through her lessons. Stay with her no matter what's a'happening!' Bodylife says to me, 'But, Blessing, she's the one who leaves me so often. She goes to the sun and the moon and the stars. Sometimes I cannot find her and I feel frantic.' And I says in reply, 'Bodylife and Soul, you is One. For this time on earth you is One. Now, find a way to be One . . . ' "

*D*uring the onset of menstruation:

I am thirteen and a half, a girlchild not quite ready to be a woman. The changes scare me: breasts and pubic hair, rounded child-belly shrinking to a narrow waist, and disturbing thoughts about both boys and girls. I am sitting in a darkish toilet cubicle at my school, an all-girls' school, and I'm wearing a gray blouse, gray skirt, gray knee socks, black oxfords, maroon tie. I notice a brownish-red stain in my gray underpants. I blush. I want to weep. How can I weep—I have only moments until the bell rings for the next class. Who do I tell? And then, I hear Blessing's voice:

"Oh Honeychil'—look what's a-happening. You is becoming a woman. You is dying as a child and now you is a woman. This is a day to celebrate! To call all the Women together to say good-bye to your childself and to initiate you into your new life and your new body. All of us Wisewomen, we'll be a-gathering in a sacred place, in a sacred circle. Some of us will wash you special, and love your body with touch and oils and then dress you up as perty as you can be. Others will be singin' and prayin' for you. When the time is right, you will be invited into the sacred circle to take your most rightful place. Then, you will tell us who you are and what gifts you bring to your Life. And then we will have a big enough party—jus' for you, Honeychil'!"

*D*uring pregnancy:

I am newly pregnant, a tiny belly forming and the first flutters of life inside. I have always wanted babies and yet have never actually thought through the process. Lying in the warm summer sand on a beach, I drift "asleep" and have a nightmare. I enter total darkness and I am terrified. The baby is growing inside of me, and I don't know how it will get out of me without killing both of us.

"Oh Honeychil', you can trust yourself here. You have a wonderful body jus' the right shape and size to let the li'l one grow. You found yourself a good man to love you both. You is wanted as a momma. Life is expressing itself through you and the baby. Look how beautiful you is . . ."

My conversations with Blessing continue. I am sometimes surprised at how strong Her voice is within me, now that I have met Her. What have I learned by opening to my ongoing relationship with Her? I've learned that my Angel of Death is a Mistress of Time. She is my guardian through the passages of Bodylife. At times she instructs me, and at others she lets me find my own way. She watches over me while I make choices. She encourages me to live more fully in whatever stage I am in. She is my Friend.

First published in *Always Becoming—Forever! A Journal of Conscious Living/Concious Dying* by Clare M. Buckland and Diana C. Douglas. Revised and reprinted with permission of the authors.

Diana C. Douglas is beginning her fourth or fifth life in one body by spending as much time as possible researching, writing, and playing in and with the sacred imagination. She also paints, publishes, and is a coach for others committed to the creative/spiritual journey.

Someday All Women
by Ruth Zwald
Fennville, Michigan

I have held a woman, my friend, as she births her baby,
so strong and fierce her focus.
Sensing her power, I embrace this longing that someday
all women will know the capacity inside them
to let the blood and pain mingle in the push for new life
that rarely comes easily.

I have walked with another woman beaten down by fists and anger
who found the courage to say, Not Again!
I breathe in her words, hopeful that someday
all women will rise and stand and shout
as their feet take them
to places where they can heal.

I have communed with another woman so old
that not a place on her skin was smooth.
Her eyes could not see the bread to grasp it,
so I placed the bread between her lips with the faith that someday
all women will be free of these bodies that betray and define us
and we shall dance to the place where we will be whole forever.

I have touched the creation of another woman, an artist,
moved by her ability to let the textures and subtle patterns name life,
swearing that she has captured mine.
In her hands is the shape of a someday
when all women will see with the eyes of the artisan
who cherishes what is life-giving and so intimate,
teaching us to value what is beautiful within.

I have visited the hospital room of another woman
diagnosed with breast cancer,
carrying the scars on her body and her soul, so core this disease.
She begins to listen for women ancestors whispering to her, "Someday
all women will learn the mysteries of their bodies and of our womanhood
as old as creation, bound to each other and the earth."
The memories of women before become medicine for her emptiness.

I have listened to the story of another woman cast into prison,
arrested for her working for peace. Costly was the time behind bars,
visible in deep lines around her eyes.
Still she says it was worth it because someday
all women will raise their children without fear of what war will do,
without dread of whether there will be enough to eat,
without constant worry
that there is nowhere safe beyond their own encompassing arms.

I have wept at the bedside with another woman, wandering in grief
of losing her partner, steadfast to each other through all these years
of "for better for worse, in sickness and in health."
The prayer I utter is that someday
all women will be free to love as she has loved,
giving themselves to others generously
in the joy that comes from being equals.

I have wondered of my own story, a woman of faith, walking a path
full of turnings and mistakes, questions and certainties.
I have become a dreamer, needing to believe that someday

all women will listen to their dreams and know in their deepest selves
that they can realize them.
So I keep moving forward, watching and seeing
if I can journey further than I ever thought I could.

*Ruth Zwald, on the brighter side of midlife, spends her days as counselor to victims of
domestic violence, as mother, as celebrant at rituals for the turning of the seasons, as
writer and musician, as walker on the spiritual path.*

Section 5

*My Journey
as a Woman*

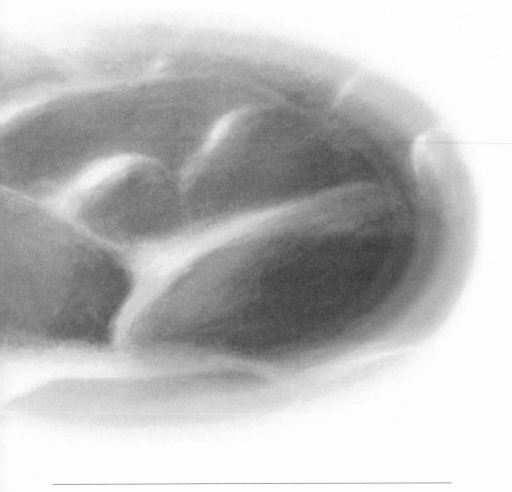

Loved into Life
by Mary Elizabeth Mason
Kingston, Ontario, Canada

I am a woman breathing, slowly and deeply, trying to keep the wild dogs at bay.

I am a woman praying, desperation seeping through the words.

I am a woman weeping, heavy-hearted in the face of yet another painful depressive episode. Five long harrowing years of recurring episodes. And time is cruel in the darkness of the underworld: a minute seems like an hour, an hour a day, and a day like the black face of eternity.

These episodes begin with an alarming suddenness and a demanding ferocity. They never come in mild or moderate ways. They are severe, showing no mercy, disturbances causing chaos in my life, both personally and professionally.

When in these depths of agony and despair, I am surrounded by circles of love, guardians who visit daily, sit with me in silence, engage in talk or simply hold my hand, doing whatever is needed. They bring little gifts of food to entice my waning appetite. They hold unbounded faith when I have none. They are my link to life, albeit a tenuous one.

Of all the women involved in my care, it is Nancy who is the primary guardian of my soul and of my life. It is she who has contact with my clients when it is time to stop work and cancel appointments. She tracks all of this in a most organized and efficient way. It is Nancy who accompanies me to the Institute when it is time to be hospitalized. And, on occasion, she has overseen the nurses' care of me. She is more than willing and certainly able to make suggestions to them when she feels such is warranted. She cares for me on all levels and is present and available to my son, Adam, as well. He is welcome in her home for meals, talk, hanging-out time—whatever is needed. For me, daily visits, regular phone calls, little treats, all offered with generosity and love.

Nancy and I have been friends for thirty years, and we have shared a full-hearted trust. She continues to astonish me with her loyalty and unwavering friendship. I can hear her when I can hear no other. I am willing to follow decisions she makes on my behalf. She is petite, although she thinks herself as tall. She is a dynamo in terms of her active care, holding varied pieces of my life together when I am fragmented.

Once I am well again, I ask Nancy to speak to me of what the experience was like for her. She returns several days later with many written journal pages about her experience, her thoughts about depression, the myths in our culture about biochemical illness, and gifts she receives from me while I am in the underworld. This is a foreign and intriguing thought for me—that anyone could name gifts received from me while I was in the dark depths. She names many. She names graciousness. That in the murky blackness, I am appreciative and thoughtful. That I remember things in people's lives so I can express interest, show care and concern. She claims there is an openness about me as I continue to see and name my experience, communicating my awareness of the dark side, keeping the flow open.

For me, I feel I become less available to my son, which is a heart-sore point for the mother in me. Nevertheless, it is Nancy's observation that I always rally for Adam, dragging myself up from the quicksand to respond to him, to address his needs as best I can. She says I never let him go in my concern and actions, not for one second.

She comments on my many friends—authentic, soulful people who have been touched by me and show the depth of the connection in their care for me when I am in need. She observes that I am able to recognize and accept my needs and am willing to ask for help—something she has trouble doing. And that help is always received with grace. She sees me as Warrior Woman, fighting with all I have to be in each agonizing moment. Broken, hopeless, bored, despairing, angry, desolate. Each moment lived as the Warrior, whether in pain or in joy. Nancy holds that, as a therapist and as one who walks with depression, my experience is a gift to the universe, one that challenges beliefs about wellness, therapy, and depression. There is an awareness in her of what an enormous gift it is to be trusted so, to be included in the privacy, the most awful intimacy of full-blown depression. She tries and succeeds in holding the gift reverently.

And so I am held, sustained, and loved into life.

I am a woman breathing, calmly and sweetly.

I am a woman praying, giving deep and heart-full thanks.

Mary Elizabeth Mason is a woman expressing a resounding and heartful "Yes" to Life, Love, and the Light. She is a writer, photographer, swimmer, psychotherapist, dream worker, and spiritual guide.

My Passage
by Lynn Carl
Kirkwood, Missouri

It was just the other day that I finally found the letter. It was wedged behind the drawer in the antique bureau, the primitive one from the shop in Rocheport, the one so lovingly restored. Often I had looked for it, knowing I never would have consciously discarded it, but always its secret place eluded me, until now. The letter read, "I hope you will not leave. I love you. I am sorry. Please do not go."

My thoughts were immediately drawn back to the trip . . . the telling trip. It was going to be difficult for me to leave my class. Perhaps I should not go. He said it was important to him that I go. He wanted me to go, he needed me to go. We would take a little time to look for a cottage on my beloved Cape Cod.

The marriage had begun with a romantic flurry. He was bright, well-educated, attractive, handsome even. He was energized, charismatic, a leader. He was an "outside-the-box" thinker. Everyone loved to be in his company. He did not follow all the rules as they were written and was a creative problem-solver out there in the world. Inside, his world was quite a different story. As the years progressed and the children grew older, I became lost, frozen with self-doubt and loathing: if only I were prettier, thinner, smarter, sexier. I visited psychologists and psychiatrists, read volumes, listened to self-help tapes. Clearly I was jealous of him . . . and I was inadequate. We became like strangers in an unconventional marriage. I felt the weight and fault of it all, and I was allowed to believe it for so long that it became true. Nagging questions would occasionally come into my mind: Why did my friends love me so? Why was I so respected in my profession? Had I simply managed to fool them all? Such a pitiful state for one so vivacious and creative to find herself in.

And now the trip. Could this trip mark a turning point?

Just before crossing the Sagamore Bridge, officially marking the gateway to Cape Cod, the words were spoken: "I have something very important to talk to you about . . . I am HIV positive."

For a second, or a minute, or an hour the world stopped. In those moments I realized I was not surprised. On some level I had always known. He never said then, nor in the ensuing years, that he was gay. But I suddenly knew that I knew, and that I had known for some time but had managed to push it away.

I remember the restaurant where we stopped . . . the clam chowder . . . the bathroom. I remember staring at the face in the mirror. I was quiet and calm. I remember thinking, "I will never look in a mirror again and be the same person." I remember knowing that something very important had happened and that life would never be the same again. And I remember thinking, "I don't even know the half of it. What will happen now?"

Days later a dear friend met me at the airport. My façade was visibly shaken. She was the only one I told for a very long time. I was locked in a promise of silence he had requested of me. All she said was, "I know," and she held my hand and we cried.

I never believed that he would really die, until close to the end . . . one of the little games I played to ensure my own survival. The illness is long and devastating, the scenario well-documented. My grieving for him took place long before his death. When it came, he welcomed it. The end of life meant the release of his pain. How could I beg him to stay one moment longer?

Through it all, it was the women I talked with, the women I screamed and cried with and to whom I voiced my fears. It was the women who sat with me in countless doctors' appointments and consultations to hear the reality and the time frame that was left. It was the women who sent the meals, who took over the teaching of my class, who did all the normal things of a day so that I could just be there for him. It was the women who came to tend the yard and the gardens, making them beautiful for me and a memorial to him. It was the women who brought the birdfeeders to bring a view of joy for us. It was the women who came to sit. Every night they came for weeks to sit with me on the patio, to be a circle of stones. We lit candles, shared quiet talk, laughter, and tears, and drank wine together. Their presence was a healing, strength-giving amulet for me.

As life was ebbing from him, mine was being restored.

Women helped me plan the prayers, the music, the service, helped select the clothes I needed for the coming "events." They helped me write the newspaper article, contact people. Had it not been so sad, it would have been fun. Do you understand?

Near the end, women stayed all night with me. They did not preach or advise. They made a place for me to listen to myself, advise myself. They helped me by being my friends and restoring my confidence. My women friends, my circle of stones, have brought me to this place I could not go alone. This is my story of my passage from need to strength, from healing to healer, my story of sorrow and loss, and of the women who guided my footsteps back to safe ground. No one could walk the road for me, but these women made the road safe and lit my path.

Lynn Carl's home is in Missouri, but she looks forward to a yearly sojourn in her native New England for the additional love and inspiration of family, old friends, green mountains, and salty air. She says, "This is as good as it gets!" Professionally a teacher and a mother, other ventures along her path include gardener, massage therapist, and now, emerging writer . . . all "hands on" experiences. The writing of "My Passage" has been a freeing experience for Lynn and an act of thanksgiving.

Poking Holes in the Darkness
by Kathy Donnelly
Eldersburg, Maryland

1 am reminded of the following Native American story:
All the animals of Earth were fighting constantly, so the Creator threw a blanket over the Earth to quiet them. Then there was no light, only darkness, and the animals continued their arguing over who could remove the blanket. Finally it was decided the Eagle would do the job. As the Eagle flew high in the sky, the animals continued to disagree over whether the Eagle could complete the task. Sadly, the Eagle was unable to reach the top. Then the animals noticed the hummingbird fly out from under the Eagle's wing, and as it approached the blanket, the animals joined together to encourage the tiny bird, still wondering how such a small creature could remove the blanket. With the support of all the animals cheering it on, the hummingbird began poking holes in the blanket, thus creating the stars. When the Creator saw how the animals had stopped fighting to encourage the tiny bird, the Creator agreed to remove the blanket for half of each day and replace it for the other half to remind the animals to live in peace.

When I found my first women's circle seven years ago, I was filled with darkness and conflict like the animals in this story. I was a full-time wife and

mother of three young boys, a part-time potter, and I had recently lost my father. I barely had time to brush my teeth, so how could I possibly grieve, reflect, or process my life? The only time I had to myself was in the shower (sometimes). I spent the first year or two in the circle cleaning my nest, pulling out strands of my life and letting my story flow with cleansing tears . . . particularly around the issue of infertility.

I had known since I was quite young that I wanted to be a mother, that motherhood was a calling for me. When I married and we were unable to conceive, I was devastated. It was seven long, dark years before we were blessed with the adoption of our first son. Then later, two more sons through adoption. As a mother of young children, I frequently found myself in groups of two or three other mothers, at playgroup, preschool, field trips, in the grocery store, etc. Often the conversation would turn to childbirth. I would stare off into the distance, busy myself with the children, or excuse myself to the restroom . . . anything to avoid the childbirth stories.

Usually, the other women would forget I was an adoptive mom and look at me for my story . . . BUT I DIDN'T HAVE ONE. This hole in my womanhood made me feel like an outsider with my peers. I felt I would never be part of the inner circle of mother-hood.

But that all changed when my one of the women in my circle invited me to share in the birth of her child. I was overwhelmed that anyone could be so generous and giving, willing to share such an intimate time with someone outside her nuclear family. The experience was beyond words . . . miraculous and healing. The next morning I sat straight up in bed and said, "I have a birth story." I called my mother and asked what my birth was like, what my siblings births were like, what her birth had been like. I started asking other women about their birth stories.

Then a new woman joined our circle, and she soon told us she had conceived a child when she was sixteen years old and had chosen adoption for that child. It is one of the ironies about adoptive families: We come together through loss . . . infertile mothers, with our loss of pregnancy; mothers who choose adoption, with their loss of a child; and adopted children, with their loss of birth family. Since I probably will never know my children's birth mothers, who are in South Korea, it was a very healing experience for me to come to love this birth mother.

Somehow after this, my nest felt clean. I began to see the shape of my life more clearly. I no longer saw myself as "infertile," but realized my life was very fertile ground.

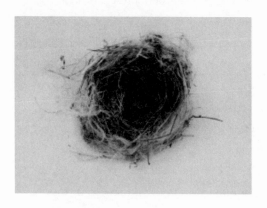

I had been sharing with our circle my experiences working with clay. Eventually, I was asked to lead our group in a day of pottery and prayer. Frightened at first, I was reluctant and hesitated to agree. Then I thought, "If they think I can do it, I will trust them and try."

From that day the hummingbird of my life was born. With rave reviews from my circle, I had the courage to approach a retreat center and offer to lead sessions of "Pottery and Prayer." The night before my first big pottery workshop out-of-town, the women in my circle presented me with a box of letters of support and encouragement. I read the letters the next morning as I sat alone in my hotel room and knew the work was much greater than any one could do alone.

The beautiful women of my circle loved me into becoming the hummingbird I am today . . . building nests and poking holes in the darkness.

Kathy Donnelly believes that every woman should have a safe place to share her stories and her inner life . . . to clean her nest. She continues to poke holes in the darkness by facilitating Pottery and Prayer retreats, women's circles, group spiritual direction, and teaching weekly yoga classes.

The Circle Continues . . .
by Debbie Capps
Nixon, Texas

How might my life have been different if, when I was eight years old, and my mother told me she wished I had never been born, I had had someone to turn to, an older woman with a big, soft lap to curl up in and just cry . . . cry until I couldn't cry any more, and she had just held me and comforted me, stroking my long, straight hair? And, what if, when my tears stopped, she had reassured me of my worth and value and had welcomed me into a circle of women of all ages, who offered me a place to go to feel safe and loved?

How might my life have been different if, as I grew into a young woman and faced the fear inside me of having children . . . the fear that I might hurt my child like my mother had hurt me, the women in the circle had assured me I was a tender and loving person who had gained the knowledge of how a child can hurt, so I would never do that to my child?

How might it have been different if, when I chose a man in my life and allowed him to be abusive because I felt no worth, one of the women had talked to me and helped me to gain the confidence to leave that situation sooner and get on the right path to a good man, who would be the father of my children?

○ ○ ○

I cannot change my past, but I realize that my past is a valuable part of me, and I am grateful for the lessons learned. I now choose to grow spiritually in my present, living each day to the fullest through the hills and valleys of my long journey home.

Debbie Capps began writing as a means of expression at an early age and has found it invaluable in dealing with her life experiences. Selected poems have been published in Our World's Most Beloved Poems *and* Eye of the World, *as well as on a CD,* The Sound of Poetry. *She works for an architect in San Antonio, sixty miles from her country home where she lives with her thirty-some animal friends and is currently working on her first book of poems.*

With Women in Recovery
by Karen Dollar
Mindn, Nevada

I'm a drunk. That is, I was a drunk until a bunch of women saved me from myself.

I was, from the very beginning, surrounded by male energy. My parents divorced when I was seven, and, unusual for the time, we kids stayed with dad. My sister was eight years older, making my brother, only four years older, my immediate role model. The only other playmates I had on the small Michigan island where I grew up were boys. I was the coolest tomboy I knew. My brother beat up on me, so I beat up on all the little boys. I found great use for my yang and little use for frilly-dress, Barbie-Doll yin.

As a young adult, I found a great yang job as a bartender, which went well with my yang dating habits. "Love 'em and leave 'em before they leave you." Get up and go home after sex. Always have one waiting in the wings. It was all about power and distance. Outer, chauvinistic power to cover up the lack of inner, female strength. I drank large amounts of alcohol at all possible times to cover for any other inadequacies that my waning male power didn't cover. Women were a species only to be tolerated. They were, after all, competition, and not to be trusted, just as I could not trust myself. The only women I allowed in my life were women just like myself, with the same belief that all women were bitches.

In my late twenties I got married. I found a nice yin male to balance my yang power. I attempted to control every aspect of his life . . . and met much resistance. I got pregnant. It happens. Especially when you drink as much as I did. I knew God would give me a boy child because I would have no idea what to do with a girl. I had a girl. A frilly-dress, Barbie-Doll, miracle girl.

I began to feel uncomfortable in my male role, and my inner emptiness was becoming more and more obvious. My daughter was a year old and my drinking escalated to new heights. I had a husband and daughter who loved me, and I was lonely as hell. It was almost another year before I finally came to the emotional bottom necessary for that "moment of clarity" in which I knew that I had to change my life or I would die.

I phoned one of my "non" girlfriends whom I had heard was no longer drinking and was leading a very fulfilling life. She brought me to her recovery group where I met, for the first time, women who seemed genuinely caring and safe. I was told, "Stick with the women." "The women will save your butt, while the men will pat you on the butt." New revelations to a woman who counted on that very butt-patting to get her everything she ever wanted! But, most importantly, they told me, "We'll love you until you can love yourself."

This was the very phrase that moved my earth, shattered my old beliefs, and gave me a new vision and hope that I had possibly been wrong all those years. There was a sisterhood out there, and it didn't exist only in recovery. It was everywhere I looked! How could I have missed it all this time? Women's pain, women's love, and interestingly enough, women's power!

Recovery is a process, as is life itself. Years after that first encounter of the female kind, I'm a living, breathing, walking-sober miracle. That "non" girlfriend is a sister to me, and a true friend in every sense of the word. We've been through hell and back together, and still grow through the challenge of relationship. And I've added many more, dyed-in-the-wool, love-them-like-a-sister friends since then, not to mention the incredible relationships I'm allowed to have with the women in my immediate family.

Today I am able to be that frilly, girlie girl and be in full inner power. I cry at movies, at happy events, and the not-so happy occasions, and am proud of who I am. Through other women, I found my soul, my passion, and my feelings. I have become a watercolor artist these days, painting the most amazing feminine pieces. Women look at my work and catch their breath, I think, because they feel that, "Yes!," that "Ah!," that beautiful, perfect yin emerging. My art is my gift to women everywhere, who restored me to my full self.

Thank you for loving me until I could love myself.

Karen Dollar continues living life on life's terms, still can't control her wildman husband, or anyone else, and prefers it that way. She earns money for frilly dresses and pretty sandals working as a bookkeeper and starving artist, while becoming a rich and famous artist and writer. Life does not change.

Happy to Be Nappy
by Natalie L. Chambers
Cape Cod, Massachusetts

I have bad nappy ugly nigger hair.
It hurts to comb because it's bad.
(I am bad).
It has to be raked.
What survives is fried.
Fried is fine.
How might it have been different if my hair had screamed!
Pleaded, "Please don't hurt me!"

How might it have been different if my hair had said,
"I don't need to be raked and fried."
"I am fine!"
"I will shine."
"I will grow."
"I will adorn you."
"I am too fine!"

Natalie L. Chambers has her childhood dream job—a country doctor. As she figures out how to enjoy sagging breasts, have a good divorce, weigh the right weight, and live in the present, she can pass the insights, honestly, to her patients.

Moondance
by Kandace Steadman
Salt Lake City, Utah

My fortress of a marriage was crumbling around my feet. As that tower of assumed strength teetered, I felt as if I had nothing underfoot to support me. An unspeakable fear that I had never experienced before and a blinding darkness about my unknown future encircled me.

One night, toward the latter part of September, my husband and I again discussed, in low-toned and taut phrases, a possible separation. He wanted his freedom to date. He was curious what options lay before him and wanted the chance to meet others before he made a decision about our marriage. I told him it was insulting that I was to be the consolation prize if he couldn't find anyone else. He left to go for a walk. It was the night of the full harvest moon.

The previous Saturday, I had spent the day at a new age conference for women, trying to gain some inner peace. One of the workshops I attended discussed lunar powers, and we learned an ancient moondance of worship. As a group, we moved with unity in a clockwise fashion around an altar that contained dried herbs and personal articles, usually pieces of jewelry, from each woman in the circle. In learned, rhythmic dance steps we'd first circle the altar, then together move toward the center, right arm extended. The steps were simple, the movement natural, the mood empowering.

Since my husband had left for a walk, I decided to go to the roof of our apartment building and moondance. Living in an urban environment, it was difficult to find outdoor solitude, but I found it that night. Once on the roof, I walked toward the front of the building, which faced a cathedral across the street. Overhead, the moon was luminous, casting a chalky shadow over the city. I looked down at the traffic dragging along the avenue. Stepping back, I took off my shoes and completed several repetitions of the dance. The dance calmed me.

I followed my intuition. Shoes in hand, I walked toward the back of the roof, away from the traffic and deeper into the darkness. I quickly undressed and began the dance again. This time, the freedom of movement, expression, and feeling synergized beyond a dance of worship to the moon. Naked before the world, my feet moving along the sun-warmed tar surface, I experienced a new liberation. I danced, I expanded, I grounded.

Later that night, I recorded my impressions: I am a whole and holy person, part of the universe. Whole and complete as I am, without a need to be part of anyone or anything else. I am connected as a woman with the goddess power and am part of her. I feel complete and empowered to do anything. The wild woman in me is whole, wonderful, and who I am.

That moonlit night, I banished my barriers and stood naked before the world. In standing up to my husband, I stood up for myself.

Kandace Steadman recently moved from Washington, D.C., where this experience took place, and is reclaiming her roots in Salt Lake City, Utah. She bought and lives in her grandparents' house, collects and creates memories, and is trying to revive the rosebushes. The moon continues to fascinate her.

The Jagged-edged Circle
by Diane Sims
Stratford, Ontario, Canada

The circle of my life is jagged. The pencil wobbles off track. The death of my sister from cancer, the death of my mom from a stroke, and my own diagnosis of ovarian cancer—all within eight months—have made narrow valleys with the sharp-edged pencil. Surgery after surgery furrows the line. The sorrow of grief amputates soul from spirit; the physical pain amputates spirit from body.

I turn to the experiences and expressions of other women who have suffered the indignity of cancer, the chafing ache of grief, to help me see that the circle can continue.

It can . . . but with different colours and strokes. As I look at pictures of myself from those twelve months of horror in 1996-97, I do not recognize the woman staring back. Her eyes have a look of emptiness, as if they were severed from my soul, dead.

I already had multiple sclerosis. Now cancer? Is there an end? What am I to learn? What am I to give?

Ah, but when I look in the mirror these days I see a fullness, the depth of pain tempered with a glance of peace that has darkened my eyes. Now I recognize her.

Who is she? I cannot but think she is everywoman who has survived the closeness of this end, whether by disease, distance, or death. What reprieve has there been? A touch of grace, perhaps, that lets the circle roll on.

When I walked the gynecologic oncology ward, cane in one hand and I-V pole in the other, I saw a sea of faces that belonged to young women. Women who had just married, just borne their second child, just been promoted in their professions.

Where was the grace, where were the circles of their lives? In the fear etched on their faces or in the pain incised on their bodies?

No, no. I could not find it, the circle was rough, torn, even erased.

◯ ◯ ◯

One dictionary defines grace as "the favour shown by granting the postponement of a deadline." [i] When we try to define grace in terms of what it is not—that is, the absence of sin—we skip over what it *is*. It is elusive, surely, but at times a state of beauty, of refined being, of virtue, excellence, worthiness, and thoughtfulness. It is Dante's anguished heart that lives in grace. [ii]

I think grace must be a sureness of step; pureness of thought, then deed. I saw it in the eyes of a woman who let me talk out my pain and anger. I felt it in her hug as we said good-bye for another seemingly interminable time. It is she who walked in beauty like the light. [iii]

I must hope that we must pass in and out of this state grace, oftentimes unaware of its presence.

"There is something in a face
An air, and a peculiar grace
Which boldest painters cannot trace." [iv]

The Chinese luncheon a friend arranged in the oncology hospital lounge is an example of grace. She thoughtfully brought only what I craved: hot-and-sour soup and the most delicate of spring rolls. (And she brought new underwear—always a bonus when hospitalized!) Another traveled hundreds of miles most weekends to be by my side during and after surgeries—what decency!

There were men, too, who helped me mend. One, a renowned musician, wrote a hymn about the worship of grace, the magic of being touched or favoured by God. My brother was my link with past family, reminding me of my mother's love. Each person moved the circle to a new place, offered new experiences, helped keep the circle moving through crippling times.

It is grace that trails the pencil back into the circle.

"My joy, my grief, my hope, my love,
Did all within this circle move." [v]

---

i. *Gage Canadian Dictionary*, pg. 666
ii. Divine Comedy, "Inferno" by Dante Alighieri
iii. "Hebrew Melodies" by Lord Byron
iv. "The Lucky Hit" by William Somerville
v. "On A Girdle" by Edmund Waller

Diane Sims, forty-three, is a Canadian whose works have been published internationally. She grew up in the north but now resides in Southern Ontario with her German shepherd, Bizzie. Diane is also an ovarian cancer survivor and is now working on a compilation of survivor stories. She also has as a constant traveling companion of twenty-six years, multiple sclerosis.

Autumn Gold
by Lorna Tuthill
Southold, New York

It was shortly after my sixty-fifth birthday when the phone call came from a church woman of my acquaintance in a neighboring town. The women of my denomination were restructuring their national organization. Would I be willing to take a leadership role in our district and become an interpreter of the new design in my vicinity?

The request came at a time when I was feeling discouraged and depressed. I had always been diligent about living a Christian life and conscientious about my education. After earning college and graduate school degrees, I had married a clergyman and, for ten years, filled the role of helpmate and wife of a parish pastor. After the marriage ended in divorce, I had supported my son and myself for twenty-two years as a public school teacher. Having recently ended a ten-year period as caregiver to elderly relatives, I was feeling stressed out. But I agreed to give her request serious thought.

Recently, I had come to realize that my life had been spent doing what seemed most expedient at each turn. By yielding to the needs and wishes of others, I had seldom taken seriously my own. Would this be more of the same? With no special plan in mind for the months ahead, and believing I had nothing to lose and possibly something to gain, I gave the woman an affirmative answer. Yes, I would give it a go and be available for the training that would be necessary.

A few months later I was one of five thousand women from across the nation gathered to celebrate their lives as women and their achievement of a new organization. Together we sang, worshipped, laughed, and learned. I met old friends who had moved to new locations and became acquainted with several with whom I would work closely. The great diversity and spiritual depth of those gathered inspired me to throw myself into the responsibilities of my new assignment and to reach out in friendship to the women of neighboring churches for whom I was to be a resource.

As we planned and worked together and affirmed each other, I developed a deep, personal friendship with one new leader who had assumed a position similar to mine. Each of us took on new responsibilities: She became the moderator for the women of our district, and I was chosen to represent our synod in a delegation of women selected to visit and partner with church women in Australia.

In all my years as a church member and officer, my work had always been with educational programs. Never had I been an active and intimate member of a women's circle. Baking cookies, preparing dinners and serving tea—the activities for which I was usually solicited—neither expressed my talents nor satisfied my personal needs. It was as a neophyte that I would spend three weeks speaking for the women of my denomination and for the Ecumenical Decade of Churches in Solidarity with Women. Orientation included extensive reading and attendance at weekend workshops and retreats. In study and fellowship together, the twenty-seven other delegates and I prepared for the journey.

In Australia I learned of women's struggles against injustice, discrimination, and violence. I saw their work to assist its victims, to serve the sick and challenged, and to speak for the Aboriginal people of their land. I witnessed the great achievement of the Uniting Church in Australia, which had formed itself from the union of three great Protestant denominations and now ministers to a population of vast cultural diversity spread across a huge continent. A burning awareness of patriarchal power in church and society and the suffering it inflicts took hold of me during those weeks in Australia.

During my early childhood, the world had given me the impression that males were extraordinary creatures. To be a boy was to be highly valued and due special honor. The question, "What's wrong with me and with being a girl?" had haunted my adolescent introspection.

The Australia experience gave me a clear and bold answer to that inner disquiet: Nothing is wrong. Everything is right. I am the girl that I am. I am a woman of faith . . . in myself and in my God

I experienced this at the deepest core of my being a few years later when I decided to participate in the Re-Imagining Conference in Minneapolis. It was there that my personal Pentecost came. Looking into the diverse faces at my table community of ten women, I declared, "I feel as if I know you, as if we have met before."

One of the older women wisely replied, "It's because you recognize the Spirit in each of us."

In the three days that followed, I was able to speak publicly, for the first time in forty years, of my first marriage to an abusive clergyman. Through tears, I shared the painful years of my faith journey through and beyond that time. Hearing of the struggles, suffering, achievements, and enduring faith of women from across the world gave me new strength and courage.

Even the church's verbal abuse that followed the conference, from the patriarchy of my denomination and others who did not accept the vision of the Re-Imagining Conference, did not bow my spirit.

My woman spirit soared . . . free at last.

While working with women, Lorna Tuthill discovered that she enjoys writing. This piece is one result of their encouragement. She lives with her husband on eastern Long Island in his ancestral nineteenth-century farmhouse. Visits to her family and her roots in New England provide much of the inspiration for her writing, as her extensive travel experiences and family memories provide the material. Time is the dwindling commodity.

Instant Widow
by Peggy Eastman
Chevy Chase, Maryland

Snatches of words, hurled like rocks, men's words. Hurled by two men, two uniforms: "Plane crash . . . wooded part of Maine . . . trouble identifying remains . . ."

Swirling words, men's words, clipped words, newscast words: "Samantha Smith, little girl who went to Russia . . . six others . . . commuter flight . . . fogbank . . . fire damage . . . trouble identifying remains . . . blunt trauma to the head . . ."

Six others. James C. Eastman, husband. James C. Eastman, son. James C. Eastman, attorney. James C. Eastman, other.

Thud, thud . . . men's words, hurled like rocks. Jim: come right now, NOW. Deflect or catch these male words. Hurl them back where they came from. Take your big, strong hands, catcher's-mitt hands, square-tipped farmer's hands, catch the words and . . .

Throw the words back at the uniformed men who sent them. Throw straight. Aim for the hurtful mouths that hurled the words that bruised like rocks.

Hands reaching out to catch my tears, to catch the falling part of me, the amputated part, the searing-nerves-screaming-pain part. Not Jim's hands: women's hands, small hands, soft hands, reaching, stroking, covering mine. Women's voices, murmuring, soothing, uttering women's water-flowing words, words that encircle.

Women's hands: Aunt Ann's hands, holding mine. Crying tears my grandmother Margaret would have cried, if she were here this day. Crying tears my great-grandmother Nannan would have cried, if she were here this day. Aunt Ann, Navy wife: Have your hands done this before?

Men's voices, harsh, peremptory, commanding: You've got to find the Will. Will? Whose will? Will to do what? What should I will now?

Women's voices: We'll find it, we'll look.

I've got it. Kathy H. finding the piece of paper, buried under a pile of scrawled-over yellow legal pads. Scrawled with Jim's pen, held in his strong, male, farmer-hand. Kathy's tears falling on the sheaf of paper she gives the men to hush up their harshness. Kathy's hands holding the sheaf out to the men so I don't have to: thin, lifeless sheaf of words bound in a metal clip.

○ ○ ○

Tears falling on hands, my hands . . . their hands . . . my tears, their tears . . . Jill and Jane and Jo and Lynn and . . . Linda and Kathy B. and Barbara and Virginia and Anne and Carol and Sue and Karen and . . . Nina and Lisa and Willie and Martha and Ginny and Frankie and Nancy and . . .

Women's hands, women's fingers, turning-toward fingers, entwining. Circles of women, a women's circle. Encircling me. Women's hands with wedding rings: circles of love, circles of pain. Must I take mine off now? Tell me: If I take it off can I take off the pain? Tell me, NOW.

And tell me . . .

How will I:

. . . breathe?

. . . eat?

. . . talk? (nothing to say, no more words)

. . . sleep? (on the side of the bed with the small depression, the place where I took up small space, a woman's space, not that other side, that man's-body valley, the one for my 6'3" husband)

Tell me: Will they call him my "late" husband now? Late for what? Late for where? Late for whom?

Women's hands, women's voices, women's faces.

Rest now, Jane says. Rest now, Jo says. Women's voices. Women's hands, gentling me down on the sofa, taking off my shoes, putting a velvet pillow behind my head. A velvet pillow the color of mourning doves, the color of clouds at dusk. Rest now. Women's voices, women's hands, encircling.

Women's words, murmuring. Women's words, murmuring of ancient comforts, murmuring of secrets from the time before time, women's secrets, womb-seed secrets only women know.

Me, curling up into myself, trembling, infolding, petals browning at the edges, shrinking. Petals that bloomed for Jim, shriveling.

Harsh word-rocks thrown by men by day turning into terrors by night: me, screaming, slammed up against the wall of a death dream. Blunt trauma to the head. Jim's head, my head. Whose head? Half-birdlike, half-reptilian night-shade creatures, ghosts of warriors riding goats, unburied skeletons trailing shrouds of death, winged-male Chernobog, Slavonic god of evil, reaching for me, a man's clawing hands, his rotting breath on my cheek.

Mother, mother!

She, leaning over me, she who has traveled all day to reach me. Mother, mother! A woman's hands, a woman's voice. Voice of my childhood, voice that reached me through her womb, mother's voice. She, stroking my forehead. Woman's hands, mother's hands, stroking, soothing. Only a dream. Only a nightmare.

She, sending Chernobog on his way as surely as if she'd taken a broom from the closet and beaten him with it. Banishing Chernobog with a woman's hands, a woman's voice.

◯ ◯ ◯

I'm not wearing black. (No! Never for Jim.) Women's voices: You don't have to.

Women's hands, laying out my beige two-piece suit, the one I wore for Jim. Women's hands, laying out my turquoise silk blouse, the one I wore for Jim: color of the sea where we snorkeled, me following his kicking-fin legs, wanting only to follow. Jim, Jim, I'm right behind you. Thinking it, not saying it, masked, snorkel tube in mouth.

Women's tears, falling with mine. Ashes to ashes, dust to dust. Women's hands, throwing flowers into the grave, choosing with me the ones that bloomed for Jim. Lilies, irises, roses, daisy-faced mums (the ones that smile). Flowers with petals already beginning to wither, like mine.

Ashes to ashes, dust to dust.

Women's hands, setting out homestyle-potato salad, slices of ham, mustard, and mayonnaise in little bowls, a basket of biscuits someone thought to bring. A tiscuit, a tasket, a basket of biscuits. Death food.

Women's hands, picking up the phone; women's voices, talking. Jill's hands, bringing me a glass: Here, take this and sip, it will give you strength. Women's potions, women's strength. Enough for a death party?

Tell me:

What should I say?

Do I have to answer questions?

Do I have to listen and nod my head?

Do I have to stand up and shake hands and let my cheek be kissed?

Do I have to smile like the daisy-faced mums?

Women's voices: We'll help you. We're not leaving you.

○ ○ ○

Women's voices, women's hands, women taking me with them. Taking me to the shore, women's place, womb place. Women's hands, bringing pasta salad and iced tea and a yellow, flower-smiling beach umbrella, bringing oversized towels. Women's voices: Let me put this sunscreen on your back. Women's hands, massaging lotion into my skin. Women's voices: Let me get you a cold drink. Holding the cup out like an offering.

Women's voices, mingling with waves, waves shushing in and waves shushing out, ancient waves, womb-sound waves. Women's voices, murmuring, murmuring with women's wave-sounds.

Tell me: Where do women's voices end and wave sounds begin?

Womb-seed sounds, women's sounds, ancient sounds of comfort.

Women in a circle sitting. A women's circle, no men allowed. Ancient circle, circle of quilting, circle of sharing. I, encircled by women's hands, women's voices, women's faces, begin to open. Listening to the womb-seed wisdom, hearing the water-flowing words. Begin to unfold petals, my petals, new petals, not petals that bloomed for Jim, trembling petals, looking for light. My hands, petal-palms up, asking:

Asking for women's voices.

Asking for women's hands.

Asking for women's faces.

Asking for women's healing.

Peggy Eastman is an award-winning author, journalist, and poet who uses writing as a way of coping with loss and grief. She lost her first husband, Jim, in a plane crash in 1985 and her second husband, Rudy, to cancer in 1994. She credits her long-time women's book club, which meets monthly, with helping her survive her tragedies. She is editor of the inspirational quarterly magazine Share, *which reaches 115,000 women in North and South America. She also writes extensively on health.*

Song and Response
by Barbara Hemphill
Kingwood, Texas

A NOTE FROM THE AUTHOR: Lee Ann was my Clinical Pastoral Education tion supervisor. In an evaluation session she ended her comments to me by saying, "I wanted to grieve with you, but you wouldn't let me." Her words held such power for me that they have guided my spiritual journey ever since.

Lee Ann's Song

I wanted to grieve with you, but you wouldn't let me.
As fast as my heart pursued, you hurried away.
Fearing compassion's touch, you fled from my kindness,
disguising your pain in such beguiling array
that only the speckless eye could witness your anguish,
could know you were terrified, alone and afraid.
I offered to comfort you, to sit in your darkness.
My tenderness you refused; you thought yourself brave.

Alone with your wounded heart, you've finally faltered.
Your fortitude blown apart by the terrible weight
of bitterness unexpressed and long-contained sorrow.
Your ancient and deep distress throws off its restraint
to look for a surer home, a trustworthy shelter.
It flees toward the catacombs, a holy escape.
Before you again are lost in darkness and silence,
consider and count the cost of hiding this way.

No refuge can understand your unspoken questions.
No fortress can take your hand and fill you with grace.
No darkness can overcome the light in your suffering.

No silence can make you dumb; it voices your rage.
My heart is a safe retreat, a quiet enclosure
that welcomes your deepest grief and offers embrace.
I still long to share with you the depth of your sorrow.
I wept when your heart withdrew; I miss you today.

My Response

Little did you know
that when you spoke that day
you spoke for God,
inviting me into my depths,
my endlessly avoided void
beneath forgotten threats.

Little did you see
that when I looked away,
your tender glance
pursued and haunted my retreat
until my vision was all eyes
and gaze with gaze could meet.

Little did you feel
that when I recognized
what I had missed,
resistance yielded to regret
that birthed a sacred shadowing
whose gifts awaken yet.

Barbara Hemphill coordinates pastoral care ministry in an Episcopal church. She is a spiritual director, poet, and tennis player, and the mother of one grown son. A native Houstonian, she lives in the Houston suburbs with her husband of twenty-five years.

Section 6

Women's Generativity

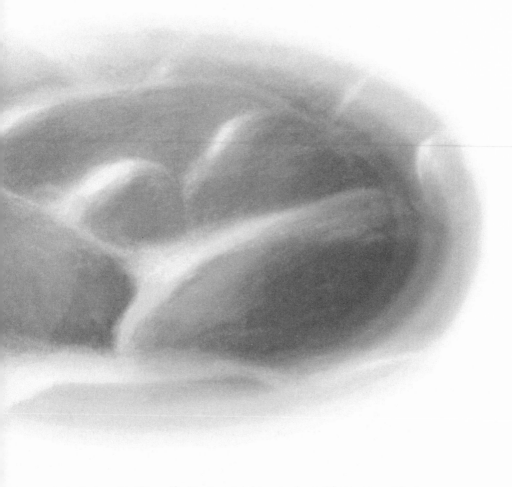

For Jess
by Patty Smith
King City, Ontario, Canada

A NOTE FROM THE AUTHOR: This piece was a contribution to a celebration within a circle of women, who share much more than the contents of books in their book club, to welcome one member's thirteen-year-old daughter into menses.

*W*hen I was nine, I visited the washroom next to Mike's Mini-Putt in the lower level of the Thorncliffe Park Mall in Toronto pretty regularly to enact my secret ritual. It was 1962.

It was there that I entered into a secret society of one, whose business has never been disclosed to anyone, until now. Behind the entrance door to the washroom was the small, mirrored anteroom where I very often encountered "those girls," whose torpedo brassieres stood out brightly against the skin under their white blouses as they studiously teased hair up and up into nests of dizzying height with rat-tail combs. Their lipstick was white, their hair was bleached, and they possessed a perfectly scary aura of sexuality that I pretended not to notice as I slipped through the second door into the washroom. There, a line of toilet stalls stretched down the length of the left wall. And opposite were enough sinks to correspond, perhaps eight in all. Seven were pay toilets, so the doors were permanently shut and locked on all but one.

I would enter the free stall and relieve myself, regardless of need. But while I sat there, I committed the illicit act of opening the sanitary disposal bin attached to the wall on my left, as though it were the holy grail itself. I knew this act was illicit because I felt guilty about it. And if I imagined my mother finding me at this undertaking, I knew that she wouldn't approve of what I was doing—any more than she would approve of my telling you about it now. More often than not, the bin was empty. When I was sure that no one was in the washroom with me, I would crawl under the partitions from stall to stall in search of discarded sanitary products to glimpse shed menstrual blood, the prized and mysterious evidence of womanhood, that state of grace so beyond my years. Oh, would there ever come a time when I, too, would bleed like a woman? Would my tubular body ever produce breasts or children? Might I one day look like a Breck girl?

Looking back on this time in my life now, I see this particular event not so much as an act of delinquent perversity but more as a hopeful gesture of a young girl in isolation in simple awe of what menstruation signified about being female. Menses was shrouded in mystery and silence when my mother was a girl, and any rites honouring the arrival of mine would be confined to a wistful glance and a simple, loving hug from my mother, alongside a straightforward explanation of how to cope with it when it came.

A few years after my private ritual in the washroom, when I became a grade seven student at Bessborough Park Public School, menstruation was the occasional subject of gender-segregated health classes. There was a genuine, but uneasy, attempt to elevate menstruation above labels such as "the curse," but mostly we viewed films in the dark that tried, unconvincingly, to assure me that I could still run on the beach and laugh at parties when "my friend" came. But there was certainly no celebratory acknowledgement pending that time, which at any rate didn't arrive for me until grade nine. Thereafter, my father became hyper-vigilant about my curfew; and while this story ends here, mine was only just beginning.

While writing this I have realized something: I am now the age my mother was, and one of my children is now exactly the age I was, when my family moved to Thorncliffe Park thirty-six years ago. And because I gave birth to boys, I never dreamed I would be in a position to welcome a girl into womanhood over the onset of menses.

Jess, how delightful it is that it turns out otherwise. As a young girl, I was pretty sure that menstrual blood was sacred, although I wouldn't have articulated it that way at the time. I'm much surer of the truth of that now. Your menstrual blood is sacred, your virginity is sacred, and you are sacred. Your mother and her friends know this to the core. The wheel turns and turns. Not long ago I watched your mother perform a private act of her own to acknowledge the end of menses, and that was an immensely moving and enriching experience for me.

So I feel doubly blessed to be able to speak to you about the sacred nature of stepping slowly and gently away from girlhood. I'd like to place my experience in the mall washroom next to what we are doing here now. My early curiosity about menstruation was buried under shame and guilt. And much as those things lend humour to the story, it was wrong. I had no female-centered community to affirm my sense of self or my curious spirit. The thing I instinctively revered was labelled and housed as garbage, as something dirty. Even so, I wasn't fooled. At a deep level, I sensed with awe what the great mystery of being female meant.

So, perhaps instead of saying that I'm doubly blessed, I should say that I'm triply blessed to participate at this time in my life in welcoming someone like you, Jess, into the Mystery of our gender. Writing this gives me an opportunity to reconnect with my past, rescue my own early experiences, and invite the young girl I once was to join us by relieving her of shame and welcoming her, too, into this very special circle. I hope you will understand your part in freeing her.

Young woman, welcome . . .
to this Place, which is yours and mine;
where the rhythm of things can be felt
and trusted

Young woman, rise . . .
you are the Dawn
lapping at our feet
ebbing and flowing
with the Moon at your throat

Young woman, look . . .
how an elder casts back
over her shoulder, calling,
"Come with us! Come with us!"
until the door to the mirrored room shuts
for the last time; and footsteps scamper
up and up into the very light
of a new day

Young woman, sing . . .

Patty Smith, who picks up her mail from a community box at the end of her street, is thrilled to be included in this collection. When she opened the letter of acceptance to this project, her then five-year-old son, Sam, who was in the car with her, responded to her delighted shrieks with, "Now, let's just try to keep the noise down, okay Mommy?"

It's Not Too Late
by Peggy M. Whitson
North Aurora, Illinois

*W*hen I tried to think of the "circle" of women who helped me through the stages of my life, I found none.

I believe, though, my mother did the best she could based on what she had been taught. She was raised to be a "Martha" in a world that was dominated by men. She learned how *not* to be a woman—unless being a woman provided you with a man. She married five times. Mom tried to forget what she felt and shared no thoughts of hidden suffering. She had no "circle" of women to go to. She only knew to bury her fatigue, sadness, and pain . . . and she taught me to do the same.

I tossed away my dolls and dresses. I thought it was better to be a boy. In each stage of my life, I put away the feelings that were attached to being a girl. As with my mother, my goals and ambitions were based on where I could get in a man's world. I thought to be, act, and feel like a girl made me "less."

After forty years of pretending, I no longer knew who I was or had become, and I was no closer to being the boy I thought I should be at age four. Now in my forties, I'm miraculously learning that it's okay to be a girl.

If there had been a circle of women to help me through the stages of my life, I would have been proud to be a girl. I would have better known what I wanted and made choices that were closer to my heart. If there had been a circle of women to help me, I would have shared the hurt I felt when abused at age eight and raped at age sixteen. The women in my circle would have told me that it didn't happen because "I wasn't what I should be" and it didn't make me any less. If there had been a circle of women to help me, I would have told them about the physical problems I dealt with each day, rather than think I had to act "all right." If there had been a circle of women to help me, I could have talked to them before my baby was born. With their help, I would have known to hug my daughter more often and to listen to her better when she was hurt. If there had been a circle of women to help me, I would not have taught my daughter to be ashamed of her weaknesses and toss away her dreams . . . I would have been in that circle for her.

It's not too late.

I can become that circle for my mother, my daughter, and for my future granddaughter, too. I can love them and let them see that they are worthy of love for themselves. I can help them know that it's okay to choose, to feel, to say, to be . . . and it's good to be a girl.

Peggy Marguerite Whitson is a freelance writer who lives in the Chicago area with her husband, Marty, and their three dogs, Dusty, Molly, and Katie. Peggy specializes in short stories and articles, but is also at work on her first book.

I Wish for You . . .
by Virginia R. Walker
Pleasant Hill, Missouri

*B*ecause I sit and listen, I know where I have been, and I know where you are. You are stepping into a space apart from me, and that is as it should be. But I wish for you. I wish for you the whole beautiful world with all of its myriad contrasts. I wish for you grass so soft and thick that your body will connect to the earth. I wish for you paths so stony that your feet bleed. I wish for you the blessings of a warm fire and at times harsh cold rain on your face.

Sometimes I wish I had the ability to shield you from pain, but only sometimes. Even as I wish you no pain, I would not wish for you a smooth path. The straight path would bore you, and you would search for the rocky places. There you would find special rocks, certain wild animals, or cold wind. The flat plains are truly beautiful only with the mountains in the distance. The flat plains are necessary. But only as a resting place until you are ready to climb the hill to get the view—to "see" where you have been.

I cannot shield you nor would I want to. That would make you forever a child. Your legs would not grow strong from struggling up a path too steep, and your lungs would not deepen and expand if I kept you under my wings.

I wish you eyes that see. I wish for you the inner eye that glows deep within. I wish for you an eagerness to explore, even if it takes you to strange places. I wish for you energy and enthusiasm in your straining, and joy in your discoveries.

If I am near, I can be your resting place, either in the valley or at the summit where your vision expands and you see both ahead and behind. I can help you catch the rain when you cannot see the sun. If I am not near, there will be other resting places—a friend, a quiet spot alone, a walk, a prayer, a song, or a dance.

I wish most of all for you to please yourself, to take joy in your own being. I wish for you to delight in your own creativity, your own sensuality, your own choices, and your own uniqueness. But most of all I wish for you to create an Eden within your own Eternal Feminine.

Virginia R. Walker is a teacher, poet, musician, therapist, workshop leader, a bit of a pantheist, and most of all a mother. She at times has traveled a very rough road and has the scars to prove it, but she also has beauty marks acquired at the top of the mountain.

The Womanly Art
by Lee Edwards
Portland, Maine

$\mathcal{T}$he art of breastfeeding was passed down from woman to woman . . . until patriarchal values finally diminished its importance and nearly obliterated it, along with the support women gave to each other. From grandmother, to mother, to daughter, aunts, friends . . . the connection was broken and replaced by a medical professional quoting from texts that placed little value on the old ways of the Wise Woman.

To put a baby to our breast is the most natural, womanly act in the world, yet for decades it was downgraded, even considered improper and inappropriate. The "Womanly Art" was nearly lost, along with the sacredness of this feminine act.

In the 1950s a single circle of women formed to support each other in this sacred womanly art. That circle grew to hundreds, and the women's voices were heard. A circle of women. Many circles of women. They meet across the nation and in other countries. They met before I joined them, and they continue to meet now, long after I have left them. Every month they meet, some with round bellies like the ancient goddess figures, some with babies and toddlers. My life and the lives of many others are different because of these circles.

When I was a young woman pregnant with my first child, my knowledge of mothering was limited to my own experiences (and how much do we remember of the mothering we received in our own infancy and toddlerhood?). I had just moved two thousand miles and as yet had few friends in a new city. I was on a quest for knowledge about how to bear and care for this child I was carrying. My quest led me to natural childbirth classes, which in turn introduced me to my first circle.

The women of this circle taught me to trust my natural instincts, to care for my body and my child in a way handed down for centuries from mother to mother. The leaders came up through the ranks, so to speak. They learned from others and in turn passed on their knowledge. They and the others in the group supported me, and I in turn supported others.

Thirty-plus years ago, the path of mothering I was about to follow was not a popular one. My instincts said to breastfeed my child, but the medical profession did not look highly on it. Maybe for six weeks, or at most a few months. Of course bottle supplements were a necessity, as was rapid weight gain for the baby. Having problems? Quit nursing; the bottle will solve them. What of a mother's instinct? What of the tears that many shed when told to separate their breast from their child? What of the sense of failure they felt inside? What of the pain their body experienced? What of the child? What of the self-doubt they felt when someone said, "Are you *still* nursing that baby?" Cultural views were at odds with a woman who chose the old way.

My circle supported me in my choices and taught me to trust my instincts, to follow the Old Ways, and to be comfortable with following my womanly instincts. Each month we met and sat in a circle, some on chairs, some on the floor, some in front, some behind, but always in a circle. There was talking and laughing, listening and crying, stories told, and comfort and wisdom given. The new members were supported, guided, and helped by the experienced members.

Reaching out was not limited to the monthly meetings. Support and help were only a phone call away . . . anytime. To answer the call of a mother in tears and help her regain her sense of herself as a woman and a mother—to affirm her ability to mother her child—was a gift to me as much as to the mothers I helped. It allowed me to be part of the chain of wisdom that is passed from woman to woman over time.

As my child and I both grew, I became one of the leaders of the circle. I moved again and began a new circle in my new home town, the first one to be formed there. What I learned from other women I passed on to many others. More circles grew from that one until there was a state-wide organization of circles that were, and still are, part of an organization that teaches the same womanly art to other women.

I shall be forever grateful to La Leche League International and its founders for those circles. Circles of women supporting, teaching, and affirming other women to honor their instincts, their sense of themselves, their identities as women, their voices to speak out. Endless circles of women, begun from a single circle, standing as a testament to women who act on their own behalf, who believe in and practice a sacred womanly act. One by one, woman by woman, across the nation and around the world, the circles spread, educating, helping, changing public and medical opinions . . . until breastfeeding became not only acceptable once again, but recognized as the preferred way to nurture a child.

Lee Edwards is a journal-keeper, gardener, kitchen witch, and casual writer of Wiccan musings and rituals. Her essay evolved from thoughts of a Crone looking back over many different lives . . . student, wife, mother, volunteer, business owner, and now business writer . . . but always woman and always embracing the gifts and power of a circle.

A Mother's Thoughts to Her Daughter
by Jo Grishman
Columbia, Maryland

Opening up

Pulling away

Letting me in

Keeping me out

So much the same inside

Yet so very different

We come from a different place

Our places meet

Intertwine

Touch each other's lives

One comes out of the other

Out of a deep love

Looking so different

Feeling so same

Deeper

The same essence

She understands we are one in so many ways

A closeness that eludes words

A deeper understanding

Only to be understood by the two

The women of the same soul

She comforts in a way no one else could ever know how to

It couldn't be any other way

She is there yet gone

Drifting away

Yet holding on

She begins the emergence

Wants to break free
Not ready for total blossoming
The bulb must still nourish
Be nourished
She gives so much more
Than she takes
I suppose because she too
Gives more than she takes
They are the same
They are different
They are one
They are two
They are a third entity
Nothing could match the bond
It is cherished
It nourishes
It hurts
How can I prepare
To let go?

I dedicate this to my daughter, the woman who has had a pivotal influence on my life, and was the inspiration for this poem and drawing.

Jo Grishman is an artist, wife, and mother. She exhibits locally, facilitates creativity workshops for adults, and is involved in various volunteer organizations. Journeying through the layers of memory is very important in her work. Through the process of physically touching and manipulating a multitude of media, a dialogue begins, allowing the image to take on a life of its own.

Bountiful Woman
by Angela Hrabowiak
Hamilton, Ontario, Canada

$\mathcal{I}$ remember myself at seven years of age, with a black bob framing my face and a world of drama in my fists. Crayon after colorful crayon was worn to a nub as I made my drawings dance to the music in my head. Miss Smith was a kind teacher. She helped my hesitant words take shape when I couldn't wrap my tongue around these stubborn foreign English words. I'm sure she thought she was helping me when she told me the sky was not green, and the grass was definitely not purple and orange stripes. She was trying to help me see what was "right."

I began coloring by consensus, watering down what I saw and felt to the hue of the world and people around me. I read cues and disapproval well, and tempered my paintings to reflect what was acceptable. Curiously though, I persisted in drawing, still sang, danced, and wrote my silly stories. I still saw magic in the dancing mauve shadows under a pine tree and still sought to capture the magnificence of the dove grey clouds towering over me. I suppose I'm stubborn.

I was thirty when I next drew my sky emerald green.

"Bountiful Woman," an art exhibition which was born in Hamilton, Ontario, in 1992, began out of rejection. For many years I had been submitting artwork to local juried art shows—and being rejected. In the typical bountiful-woman way, Renee, a sympathetic friend and I decided to launch an unjuried show to exhibit local women's work. Our friends gladly jumped in with both feet, full throttle. Then we put out feelers to other women we thought might be interested in such a brave venture. The response we got was overwhelming! Anna, Anka, Cynthia, Dawn, Sharon, Nikki, Candace, Jennifer, Susan, and Nora were there with bells on!

We insisted on only a few things: that the show would be unjuried, for women, called "Bountiful Woman," and not reliant on any corporate sponsorship. Donations were welcome from individuals and local merchants. After almost a full year's work and planning, thirteen committee members assembled a wonderful salon-style show in a century-old theater (donated). We encouraged musicians, performance artists, and poets to perform, and sold donated food and goodies, as well as tee-shirts, at a concession stand during the concerts. It was beautiful! It was overwhelming! Over one hundred and fifty artists submitted work. We showed more than three hundred pieces of alive, vital art. All abilities, ages, and media were welcomed and exhibited with equal respect, and through our sales and donations, we were able to give some money to local women's shelters.

The wonder of walking into an historic, cavernous theater, hung floor-to-ceiling with vibrant women's work is unspeakable. It was like entering a birth canal! It was a religious experience. The walls embraced every viewer with sweet sighs and chocolate kisses.

One woman, stern grey eyes commanding attention, brought her knitting to be exhibited. It was still on bamboo needles, white cotton yarn attached to an unraveling ball. We pinned it to the wall, amid framed paintings. At any point in the show, those needles could have been lifted down and worked a few more rows. She thanked us for letting her show her work. It was still in progress and she was always knitting. Her daughter had encouraged her to come, and she was glad she did. Now her husband wouldn't say she was always wasting her time!

Amy, seven years old, cradled the plastecine sculpture of her dog in a worn pink towel and watched eagerly as we carefully unwrapped her treasure and carried it to a place of honor among other sculptures in a landscape of shape, shade, and form. Her hesitation vanished when we assured her that she wasn't too young to show her work, and her mother's eyes registered relief and thankfulness at the joy on her daughter's face. Amy's eyes danced. She kept looking back at her sculpture as she wandered through the rest of the show. She came back many times through the show, and I saw her pointing her dog out to many people.

Many old hands at art shows brought their work. The art show sang with the bright notes of a soprano when their voices were added to the choir. Large, interesting, and intricate paintings depicted women in positions of strength, and the walls rang with the shouts of exaltation!

Tiny treasures also held their own in the symphony. Sweet-grass baskets, bone jewelry, and quill work tempted many eyes and fingers to touch. Quilts added dimension and texture to the show. Photos captured moments of import. Some photos were snapshots. Some photos were essays of epic proportions. Everything belonged.

Each piece of art work that was brought in with the five-dollar submission fee, and some trepidation, stood strongly on its own. All abilities were visible. All ages were visible. And all artwork was shown in the giant halls. Overwhelmingly, the comments from artists were "thank you." Many had never shown their work before and felt hesitant to allow it to be viewed publicly.

Sylvia, her dark eyes intense and her fingers stained with red paint, lifted her fabric sculpture and helped us secure it to the wall. She'd been staying up late at night in her garage with Sarah McLaughlan's voice keeping her company for the last six nights. Done, her sculpture made a bold statement. It slapped people in the eyes when they arrived at the door, with its scarlet folds inviting gentle touches. Sylvia was only a little worried what her parents would think of her six-foot-high vulva displayed boldly for all to admire. She was tired. And satisfied. She grinned like a cat with a mouse when she noticed the double-takes by passersby.

Beth and Mary giggled as they brought in their pencil sketches of Kurt Cobain and Courtney Love. They were framed in eight-by-ten black metal that you could buy for $4.44 at Zellers. They wanted them hung together.

Large black ovoid clay shapes caressed our eyeballs with gentle touch. The "Red Mother" series of sculptures were created by a gentle wonder woman with white hair, a lisp, and direct sharp eyes. Her work reflected the strength/gentleness of her character. A diminutive young woman brought in a sheep, fashioned from rusted steel, and it grazed contentedly beside a bird cage full of flower petals. I marched an eight-foot painting of bison, air-born fish, and a "cat donut" into the show. I don't know how I felt about it, but it was too large to store at home.

Nancy needed to pay for her rent, so she hoped to sell at least one of a series of impressionistic watercolor landscapes. She treated us to Tim Horton's coffee when two of her paintings sold on the first day of the show. Sarah worked at an advertising agency, and she was inspired to try her hand at pastels. She wasn't happy with the result, but the local newspaper found her piece fascinating.

All of the committee members showed something they had created. The fun was in the creating, not just the showing. Yet the exhibition gave us a focus, and validated us and our efforts in a way most of us had never experienced before. It took just one day for our wounds of neglect and shame to stop festering. With acceptance, the poisons drained quickly and the healing began.

Art is like spit; it makes life easier to swallow.

Born and reared in the Hamilton, Ontario, area to immigrant Ukrainian parents, Angela Hrabowiak explores the world with both eyes open and spirit singing. She paints, writes, reads, gardens, and collects shiny baubles for her nest.

A Healing Journey
by *Sumedha M. Khanna*
Gualala, California

I began my "healing journey" in 1993, after taking an early retirement from the World Health Organization. I had spent thirty years, most of my professional life, in a "man's world." As a young physician from India, I had first moved to England to continue my postgraduate studies, specializing in clinical obstetrics/gynecology. Somewhat disillusioned by what was principally a clinical approach to women's health problems, I wanted to explore the social and community dimensions and thus moved to the United States for further studies. The next phase of my professional career was in international health with the World Health Organization. This arena of work at that time was principally male-dominated, and I had to prove my worth by working harder and trying to be better than most men. I moved up the career ladder rapidly and reached a level which few women had at that time.

I worked and lived in many different countries and cultures of the world, crossing cultural boundaries of my own, learning, adapting, changing myself. But in the process, I was losing my own identity, especially my connection to my feminine self. In 1992, as I entered the perimenopause phase, the desire to connect with my true nature and strength grew strong. I became aware of the imbalance of my masculine and feminine side. I had become disillusioned with the man's world, and I was tired of the continuous struggle to prove my worth. I was angry. My inner voice began to manifest itself at physical level. I felt time was running out. I had proved myself to the outer world adequately. Now I needed to claim myself.

It was not an easy decision to leave the Organization, which had given me opportunities for rewarding professional enrichment and satisfaction. I was well known and highly respected. My leadership was admired by many young men and women entering this field of work, and I was a mentor to some of them. I was leaving behind a place of safety and professional growth.

Yet I knew that if I remained, I would move even further away from my true self. I had to leave to attend the voice within—to reclaim my identity as a woman.

I came to California with my partner and began a journey to myself, to *be* rather than to be doing. Living in a structureless world with no specific projects, targets, or activities with deadlines was a difficult challenge. I could sense an enormous void. I had silenced my voice for so long that I could hardly hear it myself. What was the real me? What had I lost in trying to achieve? I needed to regain my ability to dream dreams, to be still, to move freely, to speak my own truth.

I didn't know many women or about women's circles in California. So I started a journal/scrapbook. I planned to read and listen to the voices of women who had been through such journeys and draw from their wisdom, knowledge, and experiences. I began creating my own "virtual circle" of women guides.

I read poetry, studied art, and explored writings by women. A workshop of Deena Metzger, "Writing for Your Life,"enlarged my awareness to my own woundedness through writing stories about my life. A workshop by Carolyn Foster, "Women's Strengths, Women's Spirits," gave me permission to go deeper within myself in search of my feminine strength. Another workshop by Tina Stromsted, "Reinhabiting the Female Body," encouraged me to journey into my feminine self, to find a sense of home in my body.

I had always enjoyed dancing as a child, but somewhere along my professional life, my dancing feet had stopped. I began to explore my deeper self through movement and to dance again. I began to feel lighter, younger. *The Heroine's Journey* by Maureen Murdock validated my quest for wholeness. Then I was given Judith Duerk's book *Circle of Stones: Woman's Journey to Herself* as a gift by the Women's Health Leadership Program in California for my work on its Steering Committee. I devoured this little book in one sitting. My heart was thumping. My soul cried out. Paragraph after paragraph, such as these, jumped at me:

How might your life have been different if there had been a place for you . . . a place of women, where you were received and affirmed? A place where other women, perhaps somewhat older, had been affirmed before you, each in her time, affirmed, as she struggled to become more truly herself. [i]

The issue is not whether woman can achieve, but that preoccupation with achievement may deny a descent into her deeper nature which a woman must make to touch her true strengths. [ii]

Can we come to a new understanding of the feminine process towards wholeness? Can we, as women, take it upon ourselves to deepen within ourselves and each other an appreciation of the descent in the feminine process? [iii]

This was the validation I needed to continue my journey and to connect with other women pursuing similar process. I felt I had found my mission for the remaining period of my life: I must create such a place, for health and healing.

I continued to work with this dream. And then one day during a standing meditation, the name "Healing Well" came to me. I vividly remember the moment. It was like a flash while I was meditating and gently focusing on a Eucalyptus tree across from the window of my room. I visualized Healing Well as a place where women could come to seek wholeness and balance in their lives, to connect with each other in creating and/or restoring that balance by drawing upon their own resources (water) within them, their own feminine energy. I could see this place in my heart.

I spent the next couple of years studying different healing systems, connecting with other women, clarifying my vision, and confirming my sacred intention through meditation. In 1997, we moved to The Sea Ranch, a coastal community in northern Sonoma county, bordering Mendocino county. A year later, I established the Healing Well in Gualala, a small town in the southern part of Mendocino county. Dedicated to healing and whole-ness of women, Healing Well is committed to enhancing a vision of women's health and wellness, through listening to our bodies' wisdom, learning from and sharing our healing journeys, and becoming a source of guidance to each other. Our vision is embodied in the following message:

> Come to the Well, a place where you can gather along with other women, away from the daily busy-ness of life . . . a place of women from the ancient times for nourishing bodies and quenching thirst . . . a place to just talk about what is go-ing on and what is important in your life . . . as a woman.
>
> A place of women where you can talk freely about what creates health, what causes disease, and also what generates healing and wholeness.
>
> A place where you can draw deep from your inner re-sources the wisdom, which has always been there—just as the water in the Mother Earth—about the cycles of life and the healing nature of your body, mind, and spirit.
>
> A place where you can share with other women your unique knowledge and experience about your health and heal-ing from your personal stories.
>
> A place where you can learn about nurturing your body, mind, and spirit, and connecting your body's energy system with the Universal Life Force.
>
> Come to the Healing Well.

And through the Healing Well, my own healing journey continues. We women are the wells—the wells of wisdom, knowledge, creativity, nur-turing, imagination, love, suffering, patience, and power. So many of us have taken so many different paths, yet our inner wisdom always guides us toward our deeper selves.

As I move in to the sixth decade of my life, I feel an urgent need to express myself even more. Deep within myself I hold my life's accumulation of memories, hopes, fears, love, joys, and disappointments. How can I express them? How can I continue to create wholeness for myself? How can I contribute to the women's wisdom well? How can I learn to grow old gracefully while still realizing my life's full potential? I have now started a small circle of women in their sixties, seventies, and eighties who continue to pursue their life's journey with a zest and vigor that keeps them vital and actively engaged in life. Together, we will guide each other on our healing journeys.

---

i.   *Circle of Stones* by Judith Duerk (Philadelphia, Innisfree Press, 1999), 47.
ii. *Ibid*, 70.
iii. *Ibid,* 73.

Sumedha Mona Khanna is a specialist in women's health and integral expertise. As an Ob/Gyn and Public Health Physician, she has provided consultation services on public health to more than sixty countries with the World Health Organization, with special emphasis on improving women's health. Retreating from active clinical and international life, she now has a small center, called Healing Well, in Northern California where she counsels individuals and women's groups on choices in healing and integrating body/mind/spirit practices in daily life.

A Crone's Blessing
by Carlanda Green
Albany, Georgia

*W*e are gathered here to celebrate the initiation of our beloved friend, [*woman's name*], into the Matriarchy of Crones, women of maturity, fulfilled women whom life has marked with wisdom, compassion, and generosity.

As every woman begins life in innocence, we celebrate the Maiden and place on [*woman's name*]'s shoulders a mantle of pure white. We light the white candle for her, its cool light suggesting the awakening of awareness.

Share the Maiden's sense of becoming, her openness to experience, her sense of endless possibilities. She is the slim, silver moon awaiting fulfillment. She is the runneling wave born of an ocean of promise. She is the seedling pushing toward light. She is a child's trust, a young girl's first embrace. She is also the new beginning promised all women when that which has been is no longer enough. For though we may relinquish the Maiden's innocence, we retain her potential for growth, for discovery, for wonder.

As life's promises come to fruition, we add to [*woman's name*]'s white mantle the red, the color of the Mother, she whose blood carries life. We light the red candle for her, celebrating the ripening of the moon swelling to fullness, the bearing of fruit, the fulfillment of desire.

Feel the intensity of the red candle's glow in your own blood. Feel the force of the Mother as the gathering wave on its long ride toward shore. Know that the ability to bring to fruition never dies within you, for always you will have the power to move the very earth in your passion, even as you nurture her wounds with deepest compassion.

As the great cycle of life comes nearer its climax, we celebrate the season of the Crone. Overlaying the white and red, we add the black mantle and light the black candle, signifying that we do not withdraw from death.

As the full moon must wane and the cresting wave break upon the shore, so the mature grain must fall to the sickle of time. Woman gives up her innocence for the power of regeneration and creates life. With the end of menses, she passes into life's final phase, that of the Crone, knower of mysteries. The Crone is the part of us who has always known how to end that which is finished, who has learned that the *coup de grace* can be merciful in its decree, and, above all, that life goes on. As [*woman's name*] enters this phase of her life, feel within yourself the well-earned wisdom of the Crone.

Come, now, and celebrate this woman
in the circle unending,
in the circle that binds us in the sacred sisterhood
of all women who walk through waning light
on a path whose turning
has no end.

Blessings, now, on your feet and legs
as you walk your path.
May they carry you with pride,
knowing you are honored among women.
May they support you with dignity
and guide you with grace.

Blessings upon your belly and breasts
as you seek the fullness of life.
May you continue to know the healing regeneration
of your own sexuality.
May the fires of creativity forever burn
in the center of your being.

Blessings upon your hands and arms
as you reach out for the bounty yet to come.
May they continue to embrace the mysteries
that never cease to unfold.

May they hold close
the sacredness of all life.

Blessings upon your heart
as you pass through light and through shadow.
May you honor the pulse of your sacred self.
May you be guided,
in love and in loss,
by the knowing within.

Blessing upon your head
as you face the future unafraid.
May your eyes not stray from what must be seen.
May your ears not stop what must be heard.
May your lips not silence what must be spoken.
May your mind not shrink from what must be known.

A blessing, then, upon you, our Sister Crone,
as you go forth
wise and wonderful
on your way.

May the honor of your years be a light unto us all.

Carlanda Green, residing in the anteroom of Cronedom herself, teaches high school French and yoga. A scribbler of stories and poems since a Maiden, she is currently at work on a woman's book and a novel. No stranger to divorce and new beginnings, she shares her crone's blessing as encouragement to all Crones-in-training, regardless of age.

The Midwives
by Carmen Richardson
Calgary, Alberta, Canada

Today I celebrate the many women,
the midwives
who have helped me give birth to my voice,
who have listened to my murmurs,
my vagueness, my wonderings, my weeping,
who have believed in me, held me,
and challenged the awakening voice inside me.

I close my eyes and image the midwives on my journey . . .
beginning with the very woman
from whom I came,
my mother.
From her womb she gave me my beginning.
I see her.
I thank her for the gift of my life.

I take her hand
and move on through the years
to re-member the waiting women who have assisted
in the birth of my voice . . .
Taking this woman's hand . . .
and that one, and that one . . .
the circle grows,
weaving connections down through the years,
across miles of timeless land.

How grateful I am for each of these women.
How wonderful the experience of being midwife
in the birthing of another woman's voice.
And the symphony of voices sings on . . .

Carmen Richardson was born and raised in Saskatchewan and currently resides in Calgary with her two cats, Cleo and Mico (who is known by her young clients as Dr. Mico, Ph.D.). As a clinical social worker in private practise, she brings a creative and innovative approach to her therapeutic work with girls and women. Carmen is the creator of She Spirit Resources, a place that celebrates and honours woman at all stages of her life as maiden, mother, and crone.

Let the circle continue!

Author Index

About Judith Duerk

Judith Duerk, author of *Circle of Stones* and *I Sit Listening to the Wind*, was born in the Midwest of a family with strong religious ties. Judith followed the call of her early love of music and earned B.S. and M.S. degrees from The Julliard School, studied as a postgraduate at the Mozarteum in Salzburg and at Indiana University, and taught music at the university level before beginning preparatory work in the fields of psychotherapy and music therapy.

For many years, Judith has led groups of women on Retreat. She says, "I am awed by the depth of healing that comes as women sit in a circle, by the power of women keeping silence together, and by the truth in their sharing." In addition to her daily work as therapist, she teaches T'ai Chi Ch'uan and works with the ancient Taoist healing art of Chi Kung.

Circle of Stones
Woman's Journey to Herself
JUDITH DUERK

A beloved best-seller of poignant reflections, imagery, and meditations that invites every woman to honor her strong, wise, Feminine core.

1-880913-36-4 Quality Paperback $13.95

"[Judith] is a wisewoman whose words touch the deepest core of the feminine. Her astonishing insights, questions, and heart have helped me understand what it is to be a woman. . . . Every woman needs this book by her bed."—Joan Borysenko, Author of *A Woman's Book of Life; Minding the Body, Mending the Mind*

"Every page is accepting, healing, empowering. I am recommending this book to all women."—Kay Bradway, Ph.D., Founding Member of the C.G. Jung Institute of San Francisco; Author of *Villa of Mysteries* and co-author of *Sandplay: Silent Workshop of the Psyche.*

I Sit Listening to the Wind
Woman's Encounter Within Herself
JUDITH DUERK

Gentle yet provocative reflections that call women to rebalance the Masculine/Yang energy—which spiritual traditions have called "the Wind"—with the ancient values of the Feminine/Yin.

1-880913-37-2 Quality Paperback $13.95

"Extraordinarily valuable. [Judith] gently draws you into a moonlit circle of women to share their moments of longing, tears, and joy, and discover within yourself the silent center of your being. The rhythm of her writing reverberates long after you reluctantly close this book."—Karen Signell, Ph.D., C.G. Jung Institute of San Francisco; Author of *Wisdom of the Heart*

"A nourishing, tenderly understanding, helpful book."—Jean Shinoda Bolen, M.D., Author of *Goddesses in Everywoman* and *Crossing to Avalon*

Published by Innisfree Press, Inc.
800-367-5872
www.InnisfreePress.com
Available from bookstores everywhere.

Innisfree
Press, Inc.
A call to the
deep heart's core